"MASTERING THE ART OF COMMUNICATION: A GUIDE TO EFFECTIVE LISTENING AND SPEAKING SKILLS"

RAO MURALIDHAR

Dedication

To **Narmada**, my beloved wife, and our two wonderful daughters, **Vaibhavi and Jahnavi,**

This book is dedicated to the three of you, who have been my pillars of strength and support throughout the journey of writing and publishing this book. Your encouragement, feedback, and moral support have been instrumental in shaping my thoughts, editing my work, and refining my ideas.

Narmada, your unwavering support, and constructive feedback have been the driving force behind this book. **Vaibhavi and Jahnavi,** your keen editorial eye and insightful suggestions have helped me see things in a new light, and your constant encouragement has kept me going.

I am truly grateful for the love and support of my family, which has been the bedrock of my creative pursuits. This book would not have been possible without your unwavering belief in me, and I dedicate it to the three of you as a testament to our bond and the values we hold dear.

With love and gratitude,

Muralidhar Rao akkaladevi

Hyderabad

15-02-2023

Contents

Mastering The Art Of Communication: A Guide To Effective Listening And Speaking Skills

Dr.A.Muralidhar Rao

M.Pharm.,Ph.D

Hyderabad

Publisher

Notion Press, Inc.
800, West EI Camino Real #180,
California USA 94040

Notion Press Media Pvt Ltd,
#7, Red Cross Road,
Egmore, Chennai, Tamil Nadu 600008

Email ID: publish@notionpress.com

Phone Number: +91 44 46315631

FOREWORD

In today's fast-paced world, communication is essential for success. Whether we're interacting with colleagues, clients, or friends and family, our ability to communicate effectively can make all the difference in achieving our goals. However, communication is not always easy. It requires a set of skills that must be learned and practiced over time.

That's why I'm thrilled to introduce "Mastering the Art of Communication: A Guide to Effective Speaking and Learning Skills." This book is an excellent resource for anyone looking to improve their communication skills, from students to job seekers and professionals.

The author has done an outstanding job of covering all aspects of communication, from the basic elements of communication to advanced techniques for giving presentations and participating in group discussions. The book is well-organized and easy to follow, with clear examples and helpful exercises throughout. The author's practical tips and advice are invaluable for anyone looking to improve their communication skills.

One of the things I appreciate most about this book is the author's focus on communication styles. Understanding your own communication style and learning how to adapt to others' styles is essential for effective communication. The author provides a wealth of information on different communication styles and how to use them to your advantage.

Overall, "Mastering the Art of Communication: A Guide to Effective Speaking and Learning Skills" is a must-read for anyone looking to improve their communication skills. I highly recommend this book to students, job seekers, and professionals alike.

Sincerely,
Dr. A.Sridhar Rao
M.B.B.S.,M.D
Hyderabad

Preface

As we navigate our way through the modern world, communication skills are more important than ever before. Whether we're communicating with friends and family, colleagues and clients, or strangers we meet in our daily lives, effective communication is essential for success. The ability to speak clearly and persuasively, listen actively, and write with precision can mean the difference between achieving our goals and falling short.

That's why I wrote "Mastering the Art of Communication: A Guide to Effective Speaking and Learning Skills." This book is designed to help you develop the skills you need to become a master communicator. It covers everything from the basic elements of communication to advanced techniques for giving presentations and participating in group discussions.

The book is divided into five units. Unit 1 provides an introduction to communication skills and the communication process, as well as an overview of common barriers to communication. Unit 2 focuses on the elements of communication, including face-to-face communication, nonverbal communication, and communication styles. Unit 3 covers basic listening skills, effective written communication, and writing effectively. Unit 4 is all about interview skills and giving presentations, while Unit 5 explores group discussion skills.

Throughout the book, you'll find practical tips, clear examples to help you become a more effective communicator. You'll learn how to decode and encode messages, identify and overcome barriers to communication, and use your communication style to your advantage. You'll learn how to listen actively, write effectively, and present your ideas with confidence. You'll also learn how to participate effectively in group discussions and interviews.

Whether you're a student, job seeker, or professional, "Mastering the Art of Communication: A Guide to Effective Speaking and Learning Skills" is the ultimate resource for improving your communication skills. I hope that this book will be an indispensable tool for you as you navigate your way through the complex and ever-changing landscape of modern communication.

Sincerely,
Dr.Akkaladevi Muralidhar Rao
M.Pharm.,Ph.D
Hyderabad

PROLOGUE

Communication is the foundation of our society. It allows us to share our thoughts, feelings, and ideas with others, to connect and form relationships, and to work together to achieve our goals. Without effective communication, we would be unable to function as individuals or as a society.

Yet, despite the importance of communication, many of us struggle to communicate effectively. We may find it difficult to express ourselves clearly, to listen actively to others, or to adapt to different communication styles. The good news is that communication is a skill that can be learned and improved with practice.

That's where this book comes in. "Mastering the Art of Communication: A Guide to Effective Speaking and Learning Skills" is a comprehensive guide to improving your communication skills. Whether you're a student, a job seeker, or a professional, this book is designed to help you overcome the common barriers to effective communication and develop the skills you need to succeed.

In this book, you'll learn about the basic elements of communication, including the communication process and the different types of barriers that can impede communication. You'll also gain a better understanding of communication styles, including your own style and how to adapt to different styles to improve your communication with others.

The book also covers essential skills such as active listening, effective written communication, and public speaking. With clear examples and practical exercises, you'll learn how to communicate more effectively in a variety of situations, from job interviews to group discussions and presentations.

I hope this book will be a valuable resource for anyone looking to improve their communication skills. By mastering the art of communication, you'll be better equipped to succeed in your personal and professional life, and to make a positive impact in the world around you.

Happy reading!
Dr.Akkaladevi Muralidhar RAo
M.Pharm.,Ph.D
Hyderabad
15-02-2023

I
Communication Skills

"Building a strong team through effective communication: A
female mentor teaches employees the skills they need to succeed."

Introduction

Communication is the process of exchanging information, ideas, thoughts, feelings, and emotions between two or more individuals. It is a fundamental aspect of human interaction and is critical to the development and maintenance of personal and professional relationships. Effective communication skills are essential for success in both personal and professional life.

Communication skills are a vital component of human interaction. They help individuals to express their thoughts and ideas, convey information, and build relationships. Good communication skills enable individuals to establish trust, convey their opinions and ideas effectively, and make informed decisions. In a professional setting, Proficient interpersonal abilities are a valuable asset for employees, helping them to build strong relationships with colleagues and clients, present their ideas and opinions persuasively, and negotiate effectively.

The purpose of this Chapter is to provide a comprehensive overview of communication skills and to equip the reader with the knowledge and skills necessary to improve their communication abilities. This chapter will cover the importance of communication, the communication process, techniques for enhancing communication skills, and common communication challenges. By the end of this chapter, the reader will have a deep understanding of the role of communication in personal and professional life and will have the tools necessary to improve their communication skills.

The Importance of Communication

Communication is a fundamental aspect of human interaction and plays a crucial role in our personal and professional lives. Effective communication skills help individuals to express their thoughts and ideas, convey information, and build strong relationships with others. In this section, we will explore the importance of communication and how it impacts our daily lives.

The Significance of Communication in Personal Relationships

In personal relationships, communication is essential for establishing trust, building intimacy, and resolving conflicts. Good communication skills help individuals to express their feelings, share their perspectives, and understand the perspectives of others. For example, consider the story of two childhood friends, Rohit and Priya. Rohit and Priya grew up playing together and were best friends. However, as they grew older, they drifted apart and lost touch. Years later, they reconnected, and Rohit realized that the reason for the distance was due to poor communication. They had not been able to express their feelings and share their perspectives with each other, which resulted in misunderstandings and hurt feelings. Rohit and Priya learned the importance of effective communication and made an effort to improve their communication skills. As a result, they rekindled their friendship and were able to build an even stronger bond.

"Body language that conveys confidence: Two individuals sit and talk with confidence and ease."

The Importance of Communication in the Workplace

In the workplace, Proficient interpersonal abilities are essential for success. Good communication skills help employees to build strong relationships with colleagues, present their ideas and opinions persuasively, and negotiate effectively. For instance, consider the story of a young employee named Raj. Raj was a hard worker and had a great attitude, but he struggled to communicate effectively with his colleagues. As a result, he had trouble building relationships with his coworkers and struggled to get his ideas across in meetings. Raj realized that he needed to improve his communication skills if he wanted to be successful in his career. He sought out training and began practicing his communication skills. Over time, Raj became an effective communicator and was able to build strong relationships with his colleagues. His colleagues respected him for his ability to articulate his ideas and opinions clearly and effectively.

"Teamwork makes the dream work: The power of collaboration and open communication in the workplace".

The value of proficient self-expression.

Proficient communication plays a pivotal role in both personal and professional advancement.It helps individuals to build strong relationships, express their thoughts and ideas, and convey information effectively. In this section, we will delve deeper into the significance of effective communication.

Building Strong Relationships

Establishing solid relationships through clear and concise self-expression.

Strong relationships are built on the foundation of effective communication. Good communication skills help individuals to express their feelings, share their perspectives, and understand the perspectives of others. In this section, we will explore the ways in which Conversational proficiency skills can help individuals to build strong relationships.

Expressing Feelings

Cultivating enduring relationships through the art of articulate expression.Good communication skills enable individuals to express their feelings in a clear and respectful manner. Good communication skills help individuals to articulate their emotions, allowing their partners to understand their feelings and respond appropriately. This leads to improved understanding and stronger relationships.

Sharing Perspectives

Efficient communication abilities allow individuals to effectively share their perspectives with their partners. Good communication skills enable individuals to articulate their perspectives in a clear and concise manner, making it easier for their partners to understand their point of view. This leads to improved understanding and stronger relationships.

"Communication breakdown leads to frustration, but with the right skills, it can lead to understanding and growth."

Understanding the Perspectives of Others

Good communication skills also aid individuals in comprehending the viewpoints of others. Good communication skills enable individuals to listen actively, seek clarification, and ask questions to better understand the perspectives of their partners. This leads to improved understanding and stronger relationships.

"It's noteworthy to keep in mind that good communication abilities encompass the capacity to manage conflicts and divergences in a constructive and considerate manner. Good communication skills enable individuals to address issues in a way that maintains their relationship, resolves the conflict, and leads to a positive outcome for all parties involved. Additionally, by practicing good interaction skills, individuals can develop a more open and honest approach to relationships, which can help to build deeper and more meaningful connections.

Resolving Conflicts

Proficient communication abilities play a crucial role in resolving disputes in relationships. Good communication skills enable individuals to articulate their perspective, listen to the perspectives of others, and seek common ground. This leads to improved conflict resolution and stronger relationships.

Good communication abilities are vital for fostering lasting and meaningful connections.Good communication skills enable individuals to express their feelings, share their perspectives, and understand the perspectives of others. This section has explored the ways in which good interaction skills can help individuals to build strong relationships, highlighting the importance of having strong communication skills.

Expressing Thoughts and Ideas through Effective Communication

Efficient interaction skills play a critical role in expressing thoughts and ideas. Good communication skills enable individuals to articulate their thoughts and ideas in a clear and concise manner, making it easier for others to understand and retain the information. In this section, we will explore the ways in which Clear and concise self-expression skills can help individuals to express their thoughts and ideas.

Articulating Thoughts and Ideas

Efficient communication skills empower individuals to express their thoughts and concepts clearly and succinctly.Good communication skills help individuals to present information in a logical and organized manner, making it easier for others to understand and retain the information. This leads to improved understanding and increased acceptance of their ideas.

Persuasion

Good communication skills are a necessary ingredient for successful persuasion. Good communication skills enable individuals to present their ideas and opinions in a convincing manner, making it easier for others to understand and accept their perspective. This leads to improved outcomes and increased acceptance of their ideas.

Negotiation

"Success through effective communication: The importance of clear and concise expression in negotiating and idea sharing."

Good communication abilities are crucial for productive negotiation.Good communication skills enable individuals to articulate their perspective, listen to the perspectives of others, and seek common ground. This leads to improved negotiation and increased acceptance of their ideas.

Transmitting information with precision through proficient communication abilities

Expressing information effectively through good interpersonal skills enable individuals to present information in a clear, concise, and understandable manner, making it easier for others to retain the information. In this section, we will explore the ways in which effective communication skills can help individuals to convey information effectively.

Clarity

Good communication abilities empower individuals to articulate information succinctly and clearly. Good communication skills help individuals to articulate information in a way that is easy to understand and retain, making it easier for others to comprehend the information. This leads to improved understanding and increased retention of the information.

Organization

Proficient communication abilities also empower individuals to present information in a structured and organized manner. Good communication skills help individuals to present information in a logical and organized manner, making it easier for others to understand and retain the information. This leads to improved understanding and increased retention of the information.

Visual Aids

Proficient interpersonal abilities involve the use of visual aids. Good communication skills enable individuals to use visual aids, such as graphs, charts, and images, to present information in a way that is easy to understand and retain. This leads to improved understanding and increased retention of the information.

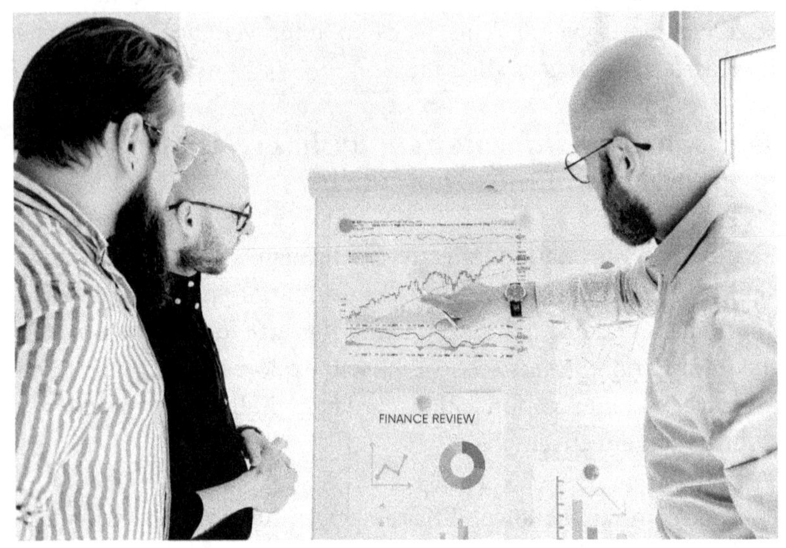

"Making an impact with visuals: The importance of using graphs, charts, and images in effective communication."

Good communication Skills are crucial for efficiently transmitting information. Good communication skills enable individuals to present information in a clear, concise, and understandable manner, making it easier for others to retain the information.

Discussion of the consequences of poor communication

Poor communication can have a number of negative consequences, both in personal and professional life.

In personal life, poor communication can lead to misunderstandings, conflicts, and strained relationships. For example, consider the situation where two friends, Ravi and Sohan, are in a disagreement. Ravi is not effectively expressing his thoughts and ideas, leading to a misunderstanding on Sohan's part. This can result in a conflict between the two friends and a strain on their relationship.

In the professional setting, poor communication can lead to decreased productivity, decreased job satisfaction, and even job loss. For example, consider the situation where an employee, Manoj, is not effectively communicating with his colleagues and superiors. This can result in decreased productivity, as Manoj is not able to effectively collaborate with his team. It can also lead to decreased job satisfaction, as Manoj may feel frustrated with the lack of communication. In extreme cases, poor communication skills can even lead to job loss, as employers may view poor communication as a lack of professionalism.

Communication Skills Impact on Personal and Professional Life

Communication skills play a vital role in both personal and professional life, affecting individuals in many different ways. In this section, we will provide examples of how effective communication skills impact personal and professional life.

Strong Relationships

Good communication skills play a critical role in building and maintaining strong relationships. Good communication skills help individuals to express their thoughts and feelings effectively, leading to increased understanding and improved relationships. For example, Raj, who has good communication skills, is able to effectively express his love and appreciation for his wife, leading to a strong and loving relationship.

Conflict Resolution

"Working through differences: The need for effective communication and conflict resolution in the professional world."

Efficient communication abilities also have a critical impact on resolving disputes. Good communication skills help individuals to express their perspectives and needs effectively, leading to improved understanding and resolution of conflicts. For example, Priya, who has good communication skills, is able to effectively express her perspective in a conflict with her friend, leading to a resolution of the conflict and improved understanding between the two.

Better Understanding

Conversational proficiency also play a critical role in improving understanding. Good communication skills help individuals to express themselves effectively, leading to increased understanding and improved relationships. For example, Rahul, who has good communication skills, is able to effectively express his thoughts and feelings to his family, leading to a better understanding of his needs and improved relationships with his family members.

Communication Skills Impact on Conflict Resolution:

Conflict resolution is an important aspect of personal relationships, and effective communication skills play a critical role in resolving conflicts. Conflicts can arise in any relationship due to differences in opinions, beliefs, or goals. However, with effective communication skills, individuals can effectively express their perspectives and needs, leading to improved understanding and resolution of conflicts.

For example, consider the situation where two friends, Ravi and Sanjay, have a disagreement about a movie they watched together. Ravi believes the movie was boring, while Sanjay enjoyed it. With effective communication skills, Ravi can express his perspective in a calm and respectful manner, explaining why he did not enjoy the movie. Sanjay, in turn, can listen to Ravi's perspective and express his own thoughts and feelings about the movie. Through this exchange of perspectives, the two friends can reach a better understanding of each other's views and resolve the conflict.

Examples of How Communication Skills Impact Better Understanding

Better understanding is an important aspect of personal relationships, and effective communication skills play a critical role in improving understanding. Good communication skills help individuals to express themselves effectively, leading to increased understanding and improved relationships.

"Building a stronger bond through effective communication - father and son share a moment of understanding and connection."

For example, consider a situation where a parent, Deepa, is having difficulty communicating with her teenage daughter, Meera. Deepa may be having trouble understanding Meera's perspective and needs, and as a result, their relationship may be strained. With effective communication skills, Deepa can express her thoughts and feelings in a calm and respectful manner, and Meera can listen and share her own perspectives. Through this exchange of perspectives, the two can reach a better understanding of each other's needs and improve their relationship.

Communication Skills Impact on Professional Life:

Career Advancement

Efficient communication skils are critical in advancing one's career. Good communication skills help individuals to express their ideas and opinions effectively, leading to increased opportunities for advancement. They also help individuals to effectively convey information, leading to improved collaboration and increased success in the workplace.

"Successful teamwork starts with effective communication. By expressing ideas and opinions clearly and collaborating effectively, individuals can achieve their goals and advance their careers."

For example, consider the situation where a young professional, Rohit, is seeking a promotion at his company. Rohit has strong communication skills and is able to effectively express his ideas and opinions in meetings, leading to increased recognition from his superiors. He is also able to effectively convey information to his colleagues, leading to improved collaboration and increased success on projects. As a result of his strong communication skills, Rohit is able to secure the promotion he sought.

Effective Leadership

Adept communication abilities are essential for effective and impactful leadership. Leaders who have strong communication skills are able to express their vision and goals effectively, inspiring and motivating their team to work towards a common goal. Good communication skills also help leaders to effectively convey information and provide guidance, leading to improved collaboration and increased success in the workplace.

For example, consider the situation where a manager, Priya, is leading a team on a project. Priya has strong communication skills and is able to effectively express her vision and goals for the project, inspiring her team to work towards a common goal. She is also able to effectively convey information and provide guidance to her team, leading to improved collaboration and increased success on the project. As a result of her strong communication skills, Priya is able to lead her team to a successful outcome.

Efficient exchange of information is critical for effective leadership. Leaders who have strong communication skills are able to effectively express their vision and goals, convey information, and provide guidance, leading to improved collaboration and increased success in the workplace.

Improved Customer Relations

Proficient communication abilities are crucial for enhancing customer connections. Good communication skills help individuals to effectively convey information to customers, leading to increased customer satisfaction. They also help individuals to effectively handle customer complaints, leading to improved customer relationships and increased customer loyalty.

For example, consider the situation where a customer service representative, Sanjay, is handling a customer complaint. Sanjay has strong communication skills and is able to effectively listen to the customer's concerns and express empathy. He is also able to effectively convey information and provide a solution to the customer's problem, leading to increased customer satisfaction. As a result of his strong communication skills, Sanjay is able to build a strong relationship with the customer and increase customer loyalty.

Good communication skills play a critical role in improving customer relationships. By effectively conveying information and handling customer complaints, individuals can increase customer satisfaction and build strong relationships with customers, leading to increased customer loyalty.

"Losing her cool: Poor communication skills harm customer relationships."

In conclusion, good communication skills play a critical role in professional life, impacting career advancement, effective leadership, and improved customer relations. Good communication skills help individuals to effectively communicate their ideas and perspectives, leading to increased recognition, improved performance, and increased customer satisfaction.

Discussion of the consequences of poor communication

Poor communication can have a number of negative consequences, both in personal and professional life.

In personal life, poor communication can lead to misunderstandings, conflicts, and strained relationships. For example, consider the situation where two friends, Ravi and Sohan, are in a disagreement. Ravi is not effectively expressing his thoughts and ideas, leading to a misunderstanding on Sohan's part. This can result in a conflict between the two friends and a strain on their relationship.

In the professional setting, poor communication can lead to decreased productivity, decreased job satisfaction, and even job loss.

"The toll of ineffective communication: lost productivity, decreased job satisfaction, and even job loss."

For example, consider the situation where an employee, Manoj, is not effectively communicating with his colleagues and superiors. This can result in decreased productivity, as Manoj is not able to effectively collaborate with his team. It can also lead to decreased job satisfaction, as Manoj may feel frustrated with the lack of communication. In extreme cases, poor communication skills can even lead to job loss, as employers may view poor communication as a lack of professionalism.

II

Communication Process

The communication process

The communication process is a systematic and cyclical process that involves the transfer of information from one person to another. The process involves several components that work together to ensure that information is effectively transmitted and received. The components of the communication process include:

Source: The person or entity that originates and sends the message.

Message: The information or content that the source wants to convey.

Encoding: The process of translating the message into a form that can be transmitted, such as words, images, or gestures.

Channel: The medium through which the message is transmitted, such as verbal communication, written communication, or nonverbal communication.

Decoding: The process of interpreting and understanding the message by the receiver.

Receiver: The person or entity that receives and interprets the message.

Feedback: The response of the receiver to the message, which provides the source with information about how the message was interpreted and understood.

Source ---> Message ---> Encoding ---> Channel ---> Decoding ---> Receiver ---> Feedback

This diagram illustrates the flow of communication from the source to the receiver and back to the source through feedback. The effectiveness of the communication depends on how well the message is encoded and decoded, the choice of channel, and the quality of the feedback received.

Source:

The source of a message is the person who originates the message and wants to communicate something to another person. The source is responsible for generating and encoding the message, and for selecting the appropriate channel for transmission.

In the communication process, the source is the starting point, and the message travels from the source to the receiver. The source can be an individual, a group, or an organization. The source must be able to effectively encode the message in a form that can be transmitted and received by the intended audience.

It is important for the source to consider the context in which the communication is taking place, and to tailor the message accordingly. The source should also consider the audience and their needs, and should choose the channel that is most appropriate for reaching the intended audience.

In conclusion, the source is a critical component of the communication process, and is responsible for generating, encoding, and transmitting the message. Understanding the role of the source is essential for effective communication in both personal and professional life.

Message:

The message is the information or idea that the source wants to communicate to the receiver. In the communication process, the message is the central element that is being transmitted from the source to the receiver.

The message can be verbal or nonverbal, and can take many different forms, such as spoken words, written words, gestures, facial expressions, or symbols. The message should be clear and concise, and should be encoded in a form that is appropriate for the channel and the intended audience.

It is important for the source to consider the audience and their needs when constructing the message. The message should be tailored to the audience, and should be designed to achieve the intended purpose of the communication.

The message is a critical component of the communication process, and is the information or idea that the source wants to communicate to the receiver. Understanding the role of the message is essential for effective communication in both personal and professional life.

Encoding

Encoding is the process by which the source of a message takes the information or ideas they want to communicate and represents it in a form that can be transmitted to the receiver. Encoding involves translating the message into a form that can be easily understood by the intended audience.

Encoding can be a complex process, as the source must take into consideration the context in which the communication is taking place, the audience and their needs, and the channel that will be used to transmit the message. The source must also consider the meaning they want to convey and the emotional content of the message.

For example, if the source wants to communicate a message to a customer, they might choose to encode the message in a friendly, approachable tone to create a positive customer experience. On the other hand, if the source wants to communicate a message to a co-worker, they might choose to encode the message in a more formal, professional tone to maintain a professional relationship.

Encoding is a critical component of the communication process, as it is the process by which the source takes the information or ideas they want to communicate and represents it in a form that can be easily understood by the intended audience. Effective encoding is essential for successful communication.

Channel

A channel is the means by which a message is transmitted from the source to the receiver. There are many different types of channels that can be used for communication, including face-to-face interaction, telephone, email, text messaging, social media, and written correspondence.

The choice of channel depends on several factors, including the context of the communication, the audience, the purpose of the communication, and the message itself. The channel should be chosen based on its ability to effectively transmit the message to the intended audience.

For example, face-to-face interaction is an effective channel for building relationships, resolving conflicts, and conveying emotional messages, while email is a more efficient channel for conveying information to a large group of people.

The channel is an important component of the communication process, as it is the means by which the message is transmitted from the source to the receiver. Effective selection of the channel is essential for successful communication.

Decoding

Decoding is the process by which the receiver of a message interprets and understands the information being communicated. Decoding involves taking the encoded message and making sense of it, based on the receiver's prior knowledge and experiences, as well as the context in which the communication is taking place.

The process of decoding can be influenced by several factors, including the receiver's level of interest in the message, their level of understanding of the topic being discussed, and the quality of the encoding process. If the message is unclear, the receiver may misinterpret the message or fail to understand it altogether.

For example, if a manager communicates a message to an employee in a way that is unclear or confusing, the employee may decode the message incorrectly, leading to confusion and mistakes. On the other hand, if the manager communicates the message clearly and effectively, the employee is more likely to decode the message accurately and understand the intended message.

Decoding is a critical component of the communication process, as it is the process by which the receiver interprets and understands the information being communicated. Effective decoding is essential for successful communication.

Receiver:

The receiver is the person or entity that receives the message transmitted by the source. The receiver plays a crucial role in the communication process, as they are responsible for interpreting and understanding the message.

The characteristics of the receiver, such as their level of interest in the message, their level of understanding of the topic being discussed, and their prior knowledge and experiences, can influence the decoding process and the effectiveness of the communication.

For example, if the receiver has a strong background in the topic being discussed, they may be able to decode the message more effectively, leading to a greater understanding of the information being conveyed. On the other hand, if the receiver lacks interest or understanding of the topic, they may struggle to decode the message and may not fully understand the information being conveyed.

The receiver is a critical component of the communication process, as they are responsible for interpreting and understanding the message. Effective communication requires the consideration of the receiver's characteristics and the need for clear, concise, and effective encoding and decoding.

Feedback

Feedback is an essential component of the communication process, as it provides the source with information about how the receiver interpreted and understood the message. Feedback allows the source to assess the effectiveness of their communication and make any necessary adjustments to improve the clarity and accuracy of future communications.

There are two types of feedback: verbal and nonverbal. Verbal feedback is any response to a message that is expressed in words, such as comments, questions, or clarification requests. Nonverbal feedback is any response that is not expressed in words, such as body language, tone of voice, or facial expressions.

For example, if a teacher gives a lecture, they can receive verbal feedback from students through questions or comments. Nonverbal feedback can be seen through the body language of the students, such as leaning forward or looking attentive, indicating that the students are engaged and interested in the lecture.

Feedback plays a crucial role in the communication process, as it allows the source to assess the effectiveness of their communication and make any necessary adjustments to improve the clarity and accuracy of future communications. Effective feedback can lead to improved communication and better understanding between the source and the receiver.

Context:

Context refers to the circumstances or conditions that surround a message and influence its meaning and interpretation. Context includes factors such as the environment in which the communication takes place, the relationship between the source and the receiver, the cultural background of the participants, and the purpose of the communication.

For example, if two people are having a conversation in a noisy coffee shop, the context of the communication would be a noisy and busy environment. This context could make it difficult for the source and the receiver to hear and understand each other, affecting the effectiveness of the communication.

On the other hand, if two colleagues are having a professional conversation in a quiet office, the context of the communication would be a calm and focused environment, allowing for more effective communication.

Context is a critical component of the communication process, as it influences the meaning and interpretation of a message. Effective communication requires an understanding of the context and an awareness of how context can affect the clarity and accuracy of the communication. By considering the context, communicators can make adjustments to ensure that their message is effectively conveyed and understood by the receiver.

The communication process is a systematic and cyclical process that involves the transfer of information from one person to another. The components of the communication process work together to ensure that information is effectively transmitted and received. Understanding the communication process is essential for effective communication in both personal and professional life.

III

Barriers to Communication

Introduction:

Communication can be defined as the process of exchanging information, ideas, and feelings between individuals or groups through a common system of symbols, signs, and behavior. Communication is a crucial aspect of our daily lives and helps us to build and maintain relationships, convey our thoughts and emotions, and collaborate with others. Effective communication is crucial for personal and professional success. It enables us to build trust, express our opinions, and understand the perspectives of others. Communication also helps us to resolve conflicts, negotiate solutions, and foster teamwork and collaboration.

Despite its importance, communication can often be hindered by various barriers. Barriers to communication can be defined as obstacles that prevent messages from being accurately transmitted and understood. These barriers can arise due to a variety of reasons, including physiological, physical, cultural, language, gender, interpersonal, psychological, and emotional factors.

Physiological Barriers:

Communication is an essential aspect of human life, and it plays a critical role in building relationships and expressing ourselves. However, various barriers can impact our ability to communicate effectively, and physiological barriers are one such type. Physiological barriers refer to physical factors that can impact communication, such as hearing loss, physical disabilities, and speech impediments.

Physiological barriers to communication can have a profound impact on an individual's ability to express themselves and participate in group discussions. For example, individuals with hearing loss may struggle to understand what is being said in conversation, leading to misunderstandings and miscommunication. Physical disabilities can also impact an individual's ability to express themselves, for instance, individuals with cerebral palsy may find it challenging to control their speech and form words correctly.

One of the most significant impacts of physiological barriers is the limited ability to express oneself and participate in group discussions. This can lead to feelings of frustration, embarrassment, and isolation, which can have a negative impact on an individual's mental health and well-being. Additionally, it can limit an individual's ability to participate in group activities and make friends, further exacerbating feelings of isolation and loneliness.

However, there are ways to overcome physiological barriers to communication. Assistive technology, such as hearing aids, speech-to-text software, and other assistive devices, can be incredibly helpful in facilitating communication for individuals with hearing loss and speech impediments. For instance, speech-to-text software can enable individuals with speech impediments to express themselves more effectively, and hearing aids can improve an individual's ability to hear and understand conversation.

Speech therapy is another way to overcome physiological barriers to communication. Speech therapists can work with individuals to improve their speech and reduce speech impediments, leading to improved communication skills. Additionally, physical therapy can help individuals with physical disabilities improve their mobility and control over their speech, allowing them to express themselves more effectively.

Physical Barriers:

Physical barriers to communication refer to environmental or physical factors that can impact the exchange of information between individuals. These barriers can include distance, noise, and physical obstructions, among others.

One of the most significant physical barriers to communication is distance. For example, individuals who are located in different parts of the world may struggle to communicate effectively due to the physical distance between them. This can lead to delayed responses and misunderstandings, which can impact the quality of communication.

Noise can also be a significant physical barrier to communication, particularly in public places like airports, busy streets, and crowded restaurants. Background noise can make it challenging to hear and understand conversation, leading to misunderstandings and miscommunication.

Physical obstructions, such as walls or partitions, can also impact communication. For instance, individuals who are separated by a wall may struggle to hear and understand each other, leading to difficulties in communication. Similarly, individuals who are communicating through a video call may struggle to see each other properly due to the physical obstructions in their environment, such as poor lighting or camera placement.

To overcome physical barriers to communication, it is important to create an environment that is conducive to effective communication. This can involve reducing background noise, improving lighting, and reducing physical obstructions. Additionally, individuals can use technology, such as video conferencing, to facilitate communication despite physical barriers.

Cultural Barriers:

Cultural barriers to communication refer to differences in beliefs, values, attitudes, and behaviors that can impact the exchange of information between individuals from different cultures. These cultural differences can lead to misunderstandings, miscommunication, and difficulty in building rapport and relationships.

For example, individuals from different cultures may have different ideas about what is considered polite or impolite in conversation. In some cultures, direct eye contact is considered a sign of respect, while in others, it is considered impolite or aggressive. Similarly, the way individuals from different cultures express their emotions and feelings can also vary greatly, leading to misunderstandings and difficulties in communication.

Another cultural barrier to communication is language. Individuals who speak different languages may struggle to understand each other, leading to miscommunication and difficulties in building rapport and relationships. This can be particularly challenging in multilingual societies, where individuals may speak different languages and struggle to communicate effectively with each other.

To overcome cultural barriers to communication, it is important to be aware of and respectful of cultural differences. This involves making an effort to understand the beliefs, values, and behaviors of individuals from different cultures, and being sensitive to their needs and preferences. Additionally, individuals can seek training in intercultural communication, which can help them to improve their communication skills and build rapport and relationships with individuals from different cultures.

Language Barriers:

Language barriers refer to difficulties in communication that occur when individuals speak different languages or dialects. This can lead to misunderstandings, miscommunication, and difficulties in building rapport and relationships.

For example, individuals who speak different languages may struggle to understand each other, leading to miscommunication and difficulties in building rapport and relationships. This can be particularly challenging in multilingual societies, where individuals may speak different languages and struggle to communicate effectively with each other.

In some cases, individuals may also struggle to communicate effectively within their own language due to differences in dialect, pronunciation, and vocabulary. For example, individuals from different regions who speak the same language may have difficulty understanding each other due to differences in dialect and pronunciation.

To overcome language barriers, individuals can seek training in language and cross-cultural communication. Additionally, the use of technology, such as translation software, can help individuals to communicate effectively despite language barriers.

Language barriers can have a significant impact on the quality of communication and can lead to misunderstandings and miscommunication. However, by seeking training in language and cross-cultural communication, and using technology to facilitate communication, individuals can overcome language barriers and improve the quality of their communication.

Gender Barriers:

Gender barriers in communication refer to difficulties in communication that occur due to differences in gender-related attitudes, behaviors, and expectations. These gender-related differences can lead to misunderstandings, miscommunication, and difficulties in building rapport and relationships.

For example, gender-based stereotypes and biases can impact the way individuals communicate, leading to misunderstandings and miscommunication. For instance, women may be perceived as being less assertive or confident in their communication, while men may be perceived as being more aggressive or dominant. These perceptions can lead to communication difficulties, as individuals may not be fully heard or understood.

Additionally, gender-based differences in communication styles can also impact the quality of communication. For example, men may be more direct and straightforward in their communication, while women may be more indirect and use more nonverbal cues. These differences in communication styles can lead to misunderstandings and difficulties in building rapport and relationships.

To overcome gender barriers in communication, it is important to be aware of and challenge gender-based stereotypes and biases. This involves making an effort to understand the communication styles and preferences of individuals, regardless of their gender, and being respectful of these differences. Additionally, individuals can seek training in gender and cross-cultural communication, which can help them to improve their communication skills and build rapport and relationships with individuals from different genders.

Gender barriers in communication can have a significant impact on the quality of communication and can lead to misunderstandings and miscommunication. However, by being aware of and challenging gender-based stereotypes and biases, and seeking training in gender and cross-cultural communication, individuals can overcome gender barriers and improve the quality of their communication.

Interpersonal Barriers:

Interpersonal barriers refer to difficulties in communication that occur between individuals due to differences in personality, attitudes, values, and behavior. These differences can lead to misunderstandings, miscommunication, and difficulties in building rapport and relationships.

For example, individuals who have different personalities, attitudes, and values may struggle to understand and communicate effectively with each other. For instance, an individual who is shy and introverted may struggle to communicate effectively with an individual who is outgoing and extroverted. Similarly, individuals who have different values, beliefs, and opinions may struggle to communicate effectively, leading to misunderstandings and miscommunication.

Additionally, individual differences in behavior, such as body language, tone of voice, and gesture, can also impact the quality of communication. For example, individuals who have different cultural backgrounds may use different forms of body language and gestures, which can lead to misunderstandings and miscommunication.

To overcome interpersonal barriers, individuals can make an effort to understand and appreciate the differences in personality, attitudes, values, and behavior of others. This involves being open-minded, respectful, and empathetic towards others, and making an effort to understand their perspectives and communicate effectively with them.

Interpersonal barriers can have a significant impact on the quality of communication and can lead to misunderstandings and miscommunication. However, by making an effort to understand and appreciate the differences in personality, attitudes, values, and behavior of others, individuals can overcome interpersonal barriers and improve the quality of their communication.

Emotional Barriers:

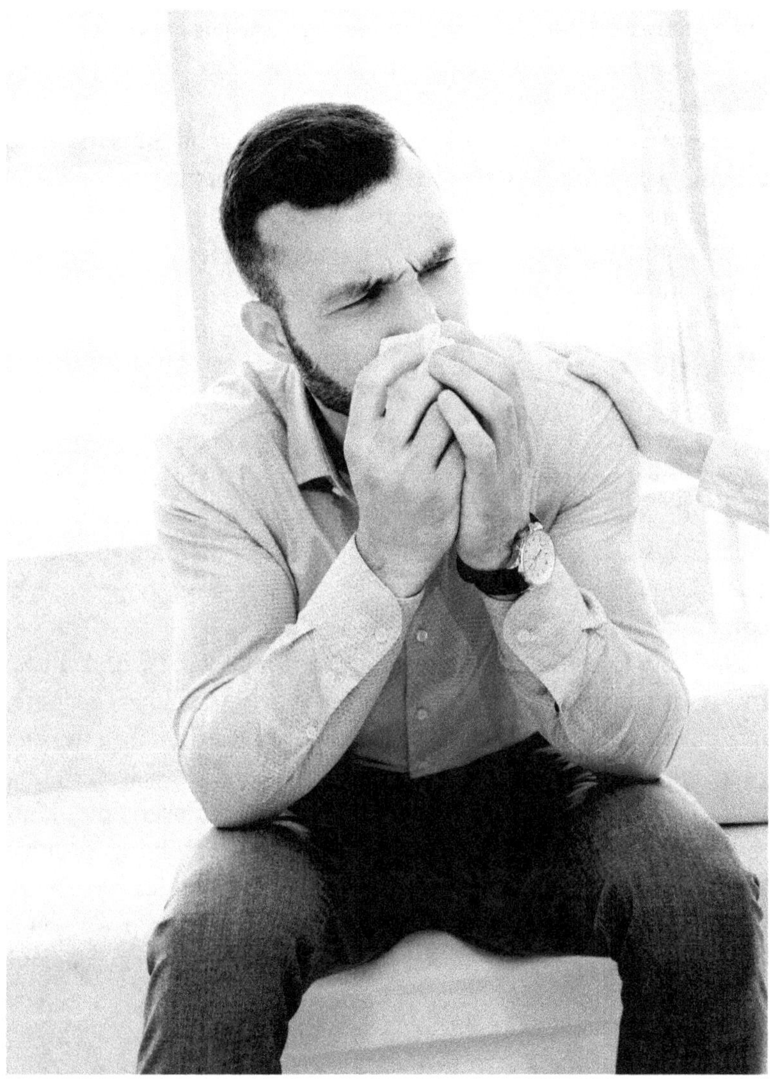

"Don't let emotions silence your voice, speak up and connect"

Emotional barriers refer to feelings and emotions that can impact effective communication, such as anger, frustration, and embarrassment.

For example, consider the story of Meera, who is feeling angry and frustrated after a recent disagreement with her coworker. This can impact her ability to communicate effectively with others and potentially lead to further conflict.

Impact: Emotional barriers can impact communication by causing us to shut down and not share our thoughts and feelings, leading to misunderstandings and unproductive conversations. They can also impact our ability to listen actively and respond empathetically to others.

Ways to Overcome Emotional Barriers:

There are various ways to overcome emotional barriers, including mindfulness practices, therapy, and seeking support from a trusted friend or counselor. For example, Meera can practice mindfulness techniques to regulate her emotions and manage her anger, or seek therapy to address her emotional barriers and improve her communication skills.

Barriers to communication can arise from a variety of sources, including physiological barriers, physical barriers, cultural barriers, language barriers, gender barriers, interpersonal barriers, psychological barriers, and emotional barriers. Understanding these barriers and making a conscious effort to overcome them is essential for effective communication and building positive relationships. By learning about different communication styles, practicing active listening and empathy, and seeking support when needed, we can work towards creating a more inclusive and effective communication environment.

IV
Perspectives in Communication

In today's fast-paced world, communication plays a crucial role in our personal and professional lives. It allows us to connect with others, share information, and build relationships. However, the quality of communication can be impacted by our individual perspectives.

Perspectives refer to the way in which we view and interpret information and experiences. They are shaped by a variety of factors, including our past experiences, cultural background, emotions, and environment. Understanding these factors and how they impact our perspectives is essential for effective communication.

In this chapter, we will explore the different factors that affect our perspectives in communication and their impact on our ability to effectively connect and communicate with others. We will also provide insights and recommendations on how to improve our perspectives in communication and enhance the quality of our communication

Visual Perception in Communication

Visual perception refers to the way in which we process and interpret visual information. It plays a significant role in our ability to effectively communicate with others and can have a major impact on the quality of our communication.

In the context of communication, visual perception can affect our interpretation of nonverbal cues, such as body language and facial expressions. For example, if we are unable to see the facial expression of a speaker, it may be more difficult to accurately interpret the emotional state they are expressing. Similarly, if we are in a poorly lit room, it may be difficult to see the speaker's gestures and body language, making it challenging to interpret their message.

Consider the story of Raj, a salesperson who was meeting with a potential client, Maya. During the meeting, Maya's face was partially obscured by a stack of papers she was holding. Despite Raj's efforts to make eye contact and engage with her, he struggled to interpret her emotional state and body language. As a result, he was unable to effectively communicate with Maya and lost the opportunity to close the sale.

It is important to consider the impact of visual perception on communication and to take steps to minimize its negative effects. This may include adjusting the lighting in a room, reducing visual distractions, or positioning speakers and listeners in a way that maximizes visibility. Additionally, it may also be helpful to pay close attention to nonverbal cues and actively engage with the speaker to clarify any misunderstandings. If we are in a poorly lit room, it may be difficult to see the speaker's gestures and body language, making it challenging to interpret their message. Consider the story of Priya, who was attending a business conference in a dimly lit conference room. Despite the speakers' efforts to use gestures and body language to emphasize their points, Priya struggled to see their nonverbal cues and became distracted and disengaged.

Visual perception can also be influenced by the distance between the speaker and the listener. If the speaker is far away, their gestures and body language may not be as visible, which can impact the listener's ability to understand their message. Consider the story of Anand, who was giving a presentation to a large group of people. Despite his efforts to use gestures and body language to emphasize his points, many of the listeners in the back of the room struggled to see his nonverbal cues and became distracted.

Furthermore, visual distractions, such as movement or objects in the background, can also impact our ability to focus on and interpret visual cues in communication. Consider the story of Arjun, who was trying to present his findings to his team in a conference room with a large window. Despite his efforts to engage with his team, they became distracted by the movement of people and cars outside the window, making it difficult for them to focus on his presentation and retain the information he was sharing.

It is important to consider the impact of visual perception on communication and to take steps to minimize its negative effects. This may include adjusting the lighting in a room, reducing visual distractions, or positioning speakers and listeners in a way that maximizes visibility. Additionally, it may also be helpful to pay close attention to nonverbal cues and actively engage with the speaker to clarify any misunderstandings.

Language

Language plays a significant role in shaping our perspectives in communication. Our understanding of the world is largely influenced by the language we speak and the words we use to describe our experiences. The words we choose to use when communicating with others can affect the way we perceive the world and the way others perceive us.

Language can influence our interpretation of messages in a number of ways. For example, idioms and expressions can have a different meaning in different cultures. This can lead to misunderstandings in cross-cultural communication. For example, when an American says "I'm feeling under the weather," it's a common expression meaning they're not feeling well, but to someone from another culture, it might not make any sense.

Nonverbal cues, such as tone of voice, facial expressions, and body language, can also have a significant impact on our interpretation of messages. The tone of voice used when speaking, for example, can convey emotions, attitudes, and even truths in a way that words alone cannot. If a speaker uses a sarcastic tone, it can completely change the meaning of what they're saying.

Cultural differences in language use can also affect our perspectives in communication. Different cultures place different values on formality, politeness, and directness, and these values are often reflected in the way people speak. For example, in some cultures, it's considered impolite to directly refuse a request, whereas in others it's considered perfectly acceptable.

Language has the power to bring people together, but it can also create misunderstandings and distance. It's important to be mindful of the words we choose to use and to make an effort to understand the cultural and linguistic context of the people we communicate with.

Example:

Sofia, a Spanish teacher, wanted to teach her students about the cultural differences in language use. She asked her students to bring in a phrase from their native language that was difficult to translate into English. The students had a lot of fun sharing the phrases and explaining their meanings to each other. Sofia emphasized the importance of being mindful of language differences in cross-cultural communication. One of her students, Rohan, who was born and raised in the United States, was fascinated by the differences in language use and realized that he had a lot to learn about the cultural context of communication.

Other Factors Affecting Our Perspective:

Past Experiences

Past experiences play a significant role in shaping our perspectives and influencing how we interpret and respond to new information. Our past experiences shape our beliefs, values, and attitudes, and these factors can influence our perceptions of new experiences.

For example, let's consider a person named Ram who has always been a fan of Chinese cuisine. He grew up eating Chinese food with his family and has always loved it. However, one day he goes to a new restaurant and orders a dish that he's never had before. Unfortunately, the dish is not to his liking and he leaves the restaurant feeling disappointed.

In this scenario, Ram's past experiences with Chinese cuisine have shaped his perspective and expectations for this new experience. He has a preconceived notion of what Chinese food should taste like, and when his expectations are not met, he is left feeling disappointed.

This example highlights how our past experiences can impact our perspectives in communication. Whether we're communicating with others or interpreting information for ourselves, our past experiences can shape our views and influence how we respond to new information.

It's important to be aware of the role that past experiences play in shaping our perspectives, as it can help us understand why others may have different opinions or interpretations of information. By recognizing the impact of past experiences, we can work to broaden our perspectives and be more open-minded in our communication with others.

Prejudices

Prejudices are preconceived opinions or attitudes that we hold towards certain groups of people or situations, often based on limited or stereotypical information. These prejudices can influence our perspectives and impact the way we communicate with others.

For example, let's consider a person named Priya who has always been taught that all people who are homeless are lazy and don't want to work. One day, she encounters a homeless person who is looking for work but cannot find a job because of a criminal record. This encounter challenges Priya's preconceived notions about homelessness and makes her question her beliefs.

In this scenario, Priya's prejudices have shaped her perspective and impacted her ability to communicate with a homeless person. By holding these prejudices, she has limited her understanding of the complex issues surrounding homelessness and has missed out on an opportunity to learn and grow from a new experience.

It's important to recognize the impact that prejudices can have on our perspectives in communication. By acknowledging and actively working to challenge our prejudices, we can broaden our perspectives, increase our understanding of others, and improve our communication with others. This can lead to more meaningful and productive interactions with those who may be different from us, and help to promote greater empathy, understanding, and acceptance.

Feelings

Feelings play a crucial role in shaping our perspectives and influencing the way we communicate with others. Our emotions and moods can color our perception of events and experiences, and impact the way we interpret and respond to messages from others.

For example, consider a person named Ravi who has had a long and stressful day at work. He arrives home to find that his spouse, Maya, has planned a surprise dinner party for their friends. Despite the good intentions of Maya, Ravi's mood and feelings about his day cause him to perceive the situation as overwhelming and annoying. This, in turn, influences his communication with Maya, leading to frustration and misunderstandings.

It's important to be aware of the impact that our feelings can have on our perspectives and communication with others. By taking the time to manage our emotions and regulate our mood, we can gain greater control over the way we perceive and respond to situations and messages from others. This can help to improve the quality and effectiveness of our communication, and lead to more positive and productive relationships with others.

Feelings play a significant role in shaping our perspectives and influencing the way we communicate with others. By recognizing and managing the impact of our emotions, we can gain greater control over our perspectives and improve the effectiveness of our communication with others.

Environment

The environment in which we find ourselves can also have a significant impact on our perspectives and the way we communicate with others. Our surroundings, including the physical space, social context, and cultural norms, can all shape our perceptions and influence the way we respond to messages and situations.

For example, consider a young woman named Priya who works in a traditional corporate office environment. Despite her enthusiasm for her job, she may feel frustrated by the rigid hierarchical structure and conservative cultural norms of her workplace. This may influence the way she communicates with her colleagues and superiors, leading to a feeling of disconnection and dissatisfaction.

In contrast, imagine a person named Arjun who works in a more collaborative and open environment, where creativity and innovation are valued. Arjun is likely to have a more positive and empowering perspective, which will influence his communication with others in a more positive and productive way.

It's important to be aware of the impact that our environment can have on our perspectives and communication with others. By making a conscious effort to surround ourselves with positive and supportive people, and to create an environment that supports our goals and values, we can enhance our perspectives and improve the quality of our communication with others.

The environment in which we find ourselves can play a significant role in shaping our perspectives and influencing the way we communicate with others. By being mindful of the impact of our surroundings, and making an effort to create a positive and supportive environment, we can improve the effectiveness of our communication with others and lead more fulfilling and satisfying lives.

V
Elements of Communication

Introduction

Communication can be defined as the exchange of information, ideas, opinions or feelings between individuals through a common medium. It can occur through various forms such as verbal, nonverbal, written or visual.

Examples of the Importance of Communication:

Personal Relationships: Communication is the foundation of any strong personal relationship. It enables partners to express their thoughts and feelings, understand each other's perspectives, and resolve conflicts effectively. For instance, consider the story of Rohit and Priya, a married couple in India. When Rohit was unhappy about something, instead of talking about it with Priya, he would withdraw and ignore her. This created misunderstandings and hurt feelings between them. However, after they learned the importance of effective communication and made an effort to listen to each other and express their feelings, their relationship became stronger.

Professional Settings: In the workplace, effective communication is necessary for teamwork, collaboration, and achieving goals. For instance, consider the story of Raj, a project manager at a software company. When he didn't communicate clearly with his team, project deadlines were missed, and team members felt frustrated. However, after he learned the importance of clear and concise communication, he was able to communicate project goals and expectations effectively, leading to improved collaboration and increased productivity.

Conflict Resolution: Communication is also important in resolving conflicts and disagreements. By listening to each other, expressing concerns and negotiating effectively, individuals can find mutually beneficial solutions to problems. For example, consider the story of two business partners, Sanjay and Anjali. When they had disagreements about the direction of their company, they used to argue and become defensive. However, after they learned the importance of effective communication in conflict resolution, they were able to listen to each other, express their concerns, and find solutions that worked for both of them.

These examples demonstrate the importance of communication in various aspects of our lives and highlight how effective communication can lead to better relationships, improved teamwork and productivity, and successful conflict resolution.

The Different Forms of Communication:

Verbal Communication: Verbal communication involves the use of spoken words to exchange information. It can take place in person, over the phone, or through other technology such as video conferencing. This form of communication is further divided into two types: oral and written. Oral communication involves speaking face-to-face or over the phone, while written communication involves written text, such as emails, letters, or reports.

Nonverbal Communication: Nonverbal communication involves the use of nonverbal cues, such as gestures, facial expressions, posture, and body language, to convey information. This form of communication is often referred to as "body language" and can be used to complement, emphasize, or contradict verbal communication. For example, a smile can indicate agreement or happiness, while crossed arms can indicate defensiveness or disagreement.

" A man with a questioning expression: Silent gestures, expressions, and postures can reveal more than spoken words. Learning to read nonverbal cues is a valuable skill in both personal and professional relationships."

Written Communication: Written communication involves written text, such as emails, letters, memos, or reports. This form of communication is often used in professional settings to convey information in a permanent, documented form. It is important to be clear and concise in written communication to ensure that the message is understood correctly.

Visual Communication: Visual communication involves the use of images, charts, graphs, videos, or other visual aids to convey information. This form of communication can be especially effective in conveying complex information in an engaging and easily digestible form. For example, a chart or graph can help to visualize data in a way that is easy to understand.

It is important to understand and utilize different forms of communication in order to effectively convey information and ideas in various situations. Verbal, nonverbal, written, and visual communication each have their own strengths and weaknesses, and the most appropriate form of communication will depend on the specific context and the information being conveyed.

Face-to-Face Communication

Face-to-face communication is the most direct form of communication, in which two or more individuals communicate in each other's presence. This type of communication is characterized by the use of spoken words, body language, and other nonverbal cues, such as gestures and facial expressions.

Face-to-face communication is often considered the most effective form of communication, as it allows individuals to exchange information and ideas in real-time and with immediate feedback. This type of communication is particularly important in building and maintaining personal relationships, as well as in professional settings where trust, understanding, and collaboration are key.

For example, consider the story of Raj and Priya, who are co-workers at a software company. When they had to discuss a complicated project, they scheduled a face-to-face meeting to ensure that they were able to understand each other's perspectives and make a plan together. During the meeting, they were able to ask questions, clarify misunderstandings, and reach a mutual understanding about the project.

Face-to-face communication is a crucial component of effective communication and should not be overlooked, especially in situations where clear understanding and collaboration are important. By using this type of communication, individuals are able to build trust, resolve misunderstandings, and achieve their goals more effectively.

Tone of Voice:

The tone of voice is an important aspect of verbal communication, as it conveys emotions, attitudes, and intentions. The tone of voice can greatly impact the meaning and effectiveness of a message, and it can be used to complement, emphasize, or contradict verbal communication.

For example, consider the story of Ravi and Neha, who were discussing a problem at work. Ravi approached the conversation with a calm and neutral tone, while Neha was visibly upset and used a sharp and aggressive tone. Their different tones of voice conveyed their emotions and attitudes towards the situation, and affected the outcome of their conversation.

It is important to be aware of the tone of voice being used in communication, as well as to understand how it can impact the meaning and effectiveness of a message. For effective communication, it is often helpful to use a tone that is appropriate for the situation and the audience, and to be mindful of how one's tone of voice may be perceived.

The tone of voice is a critical component of verbal communication, and can greatly impact the meaning and effectiveness of a message. By being aware of the tone of voice being used and how it can impact communication, individuals can improve their ability to communicate effectively in various situations.

Importance of Tone:

The tone of voice used in communication is an important factor that can greatly impact the meaning and effectiveness of a message. The tone of voice can convey emotions, attitudes, and intentions, and can affect how a message is received by the listener.

For example, consider the story of Mukesh and Sita, who were having a disagreement about a project at work. Mukesh approached the conversation with a friendly and supportive tone, while Sita used a critical and confrontational tone. Their different tones of voice conveyed their emotions and attitudes towards the situation, and affected the outcome of their conversation.

Effective communication requires the use of an appropriate tone of voice that matches the situation and the audience. The tone of voice can also be used to emphasize, complement, or contradict verbal communication, making it an important tool for communicating effectively and persuasively.

In conclusion, the tone of voice is a critical aspect of effective communication, and it is important to be aware of how it can impact the meaning and effectiveness of a message. By using an appropriate tone of voice and being mindful of how it may be perceived, individuals can improve their ability to communicate effectively and achieve their goals.

Some common types of tone include:

Neutral Tone: A neutral tone is used when conveying information or making statements without expressing any particular emotion or attitude.

Sarcastic Tone: A sarcastic tone is used to express irony, sarcasm, or disbelief, often by using a tone that is opposite to the actual meaning of the words.

Enthusiastic Tone: An enthusiastic tone is used to express excitement, interest, or positive emotion, often by using a lively and energetic tone of voice.

Angry Tone: An angry tone is used to express frustration, annoyance, or anger, often by using a raised or forceful tone of voice.

Sad Tone: A sad tone is used to express sadness, disappointment, or grief, often by using a quiet or melancholic tone of voice.

These are just a few examples of the different types of tone that can be used in communication. The tone of voice used can greatly impact the meaning and effectiveness of a message, and it is important to be aware of how it may be perceived by the listener.

The tone of voice is a critical aspect of effective communication, and it is important to understand the different types of tone and how they can impact the meaning and effectiveness of a message. By being mindful of the tone of voice being used and how it may be perceived, individuals can improve their ability to communicate effectively in various situations.

Neutral Tone:

A neutral tone is used when conveying information or making statements without expressing any particular emotion or attitude. It is often used when the speaker wants to present the information objectively, without any bias or emotional influence. A neutral tone can also be used to convey information in a calm and professional manner, such as in a business setting.

For example, consider the story of Rajesh, who was delivering a presentation to his colleagues. He used a neutral tone throughout the presentation, focusing on delivering the information accurately and objectively. By using a neutral tone, Rajesh was able to convey the information clearly and effectively, without any distractions or biases from his emotions.

A neutral tone can be an effective tool for communicating information in a clear and objective manner, and it can also help to build trust and credibility with the listener. However, it is important to be aware of the tone of voice being used, as a neutral tone may also be perceived as lacking in enthusiasm or emotion.

The neutral tone is an important form of tone that can be used to convey information objectively and effectively, particularly in formal or professional settings. By using a neutral tone, individuals can improve their ability to communicate information accurately and without bias, and to build trust and credibility with their audience

Sarcastic Tone:

"The tone of voice can make all the difference, adding humor or sarcasm to a message can change its meaning completely."

A sarcastic tone is used to express irony, sarcasm, or disbelief, often by using a tone that is opposite to the actual meaning of the words. This type of tone is used to convey a message that is different from the literal meaning of the words being spoken.

For example, consider the story of Priya, who was talking to her friend about a bad movie they had just watched. Priya used a sarcastic tone to express her disappointment with the movie, saying things like "Wow, that was really good" or "I'm sure this will win an Oscar." By using a sarcastic tone, Priya was able to convey her disappointment in an entertaining and lighthearted manner.

A sarcastic tone can be an effective tool for communicating a message in a humorous or lighthearted way, and it can also help to diffuse tense or difficult situations. However, it is important to be mindful of the tone being used, as sarcasm can also be misinterpreted or taken the wrong way, leading to confusion or offense.

The sarcastic tone is a form of tone that can be used to express irony, sarcasm, or disbelief in a humorous or lighthearted manner. By being mindful of the tone being used and how it may be perceived, individuals can use sarcasm to effectively communicate their message and diffuse difficult situations.

Enthusiastic Tone:

An enthusiastic tone is used to express excitement, energy, and positive emotion. It is characterized by an energetic and upbeat tone of voice, and is often used to convey a message of excitement, interest, or positive energy.

For example, consider the story of Mukesh, who was presenting a new business idea to his team. Mukesh used an enthusiastic tone throughout the presentation, conveying his excitement about the idea and the potential for success. By using an enthusiastic tone, Mukesh was able to engage his audience and convey his passion for the project.

An enthusiastic tone can be an effective tool for communicating a message in an engaging and motivating way. It can also help to build rapport with the listener and create a positive and energetic atmosphere. However, it is important to be aware of the tone being used, as an overly enthusiastic tone can be perceived as fake or insincere.

The enthusiastic tone is an important form of tone that can be used to express excitement, energy, and positive emotion. By using an enthusiastic tone in an appropriate manner, individuals can improve their ability to communicate in an engaging and motivating way, and to build rapport with their audience.

Angry Tone:

An angry tone is used to express anger, frustration, or annoyance. It is characterized by a harsh, sharp, and sometimes loud tone of voice, and is often used to communicate feelings of anger or frustration.

For example, consider the story of Rohit, who was frustrated with the poor service he received at a restaurant. Rohit used an angry tone when speaking to the manager, expressing his dissatisfaction with the service and the poor quality of the food. By using an angry tone, Rohit was able to communicate his feelings of frustration and make his concerns known.

An angry tone can be an effective tool for communicating a message when used appropriately, as it can help to convey a sense of urgency or importance. However, it is important to be mindful of the tone being used, as an angry tone can be perceived as aggressive or hostile, leading to confusion or offense.

The angry tone is a form of tone that can be used to express anger, frustration, or annoyance. By being mindful of the tone being used and how it may be perceived, individuals can use an angry tone in an appropriate manner to effectively communicate their message and express their concerns.

Sad Tone

A sad tone is used to express sadness, disappointment, or grief. It is characterized by a soft, slow, and sometimes low tone of voice, and is often used to communicate feelings of sadness or disappointment.

For example, consider the story of Priya, who received sad news about the loss of a loved one. Priya used a sad tone when speaking about the loss, expressing her grief and sadness about the situation. By using a sad tone, Priya was able to communicate her emotions and offer support to others who may also be grieving.

A sad tone can be an effective tool for communicating empathy and compassion, and for expressing deep sadness or disappointment. However, it is important to be mindful of the tone being used, as a sad tone can be perceived as hopeless or negative, leading to a lack of motivation or support.

The sad tone is a form of tone that can be used to express sadness, disappointment, or grief. By using a sad tone in an appropriate manner, individuals can communicate their emotions and offer support to others who may also be grieving. However, it is important to be mindful of the tone being used, as a sad tone can also have negative effects.

Techniques for Improving Tone:

Improving the tone of voice used in communication can greatly enhance the effectiveness and clarity of the message being conveyed. Here are some techniques that can be used to improve tone:

Practice active listening: Active listening involves paying close attention to the tone and body language of the person speaking, and using that information to respond in a manner that is appropriate and empathetic.

Control your breathing: Taking deep breaths and slowing down the pace of breathing can help to regulate the tone of voice and reduce stress or anxiety.

Be aware of your body language: Body language can greatly impact the tone of voice used in communication. By being aware of and controlling body language, individuals can project a more confident and relaxed tone.

Pay attention to your tone: Being mindful of the tone of voice used in communication can help to identify areas for improvement and to make necessary adjustments.

Practice speaking in different tones: Practicing speaking in different tones, such as a happy or sad tone, can help to improve the overall tone used in communication and increase the ability to effectively convey emotions.

Improving the tone of voice used in communication is an important aspect of effective communication. By using techniques such as active listening, controlling breathing and body language, being aware of tone, and practicing speaking in different tones, individuals can improve their tone and enhance the clarity and effectiveness of their message.

Body Language (Non-Verbal Communication)

Body language, also known as non-verbal communication, refers to the way in which individuals communicate through their posture, gestures, and facial expressions, as well as through their use of space and touch. Body language plays a significant role in the way in which a message is perceived and can greatly enhance or detract from the meaning of the message being conveyed.

Importance of Body Language:

Body language is an important aspect of communication, as it can convey information that is not communicated through words. For example, a smile or a nod of the head can indicate agreement or approval, while crossed arms or a furrowed brow can indicate discomfort or disagreement.

Types of Body Language:

There are many different types of body language, including facial expressions, gestures, posture, and the use of space and touch. Some common forms of body language include:

Facial expressions: The way in which an individual's face is animated can convey a range of emotions, from happiness and excitement to sadness and anger.

Gestures: Gestures, such as pointing, nodding, or waving, can convey information and express emotions.

Posture: An individual's posture can indicate their level of confidence, their mood, and their level of attentiveness.

Use of space and touch: The way in which individuals use space and touch in communication can also convey information and express emotions.

Body language, or non-verbal communication, is a crucial aspect of communication that can greatly enhance or detract from the message being conveyed. Understanding the various forms of body language and paying attention to non-verbal cues can greatly improve the effectiveness of communication in personal and professional settings.

Techniques for Improving Non-Verbal Communication

Improving non-verbal communication, or body language, can greatly enhance the effectiveness and clarity of the message being conveyed. Here are some techniques that can be used to improve non-verbal communication:

Observe others: Paying close attention to the body language of others can help to identify the types of non-verbal cues that are most effective in conveying emotions and information.

Practice active listening: Active listening involves paying close attention to the tone and body language of the person speaking, and using that information to respond in a manner that is appropriate and empathetic.

Be aware of your own body language: Being mindful of one's own body language can help to identify areas for improvement and to make necessary adjustments.

Practice good posture: Good posture can convey confidence and attentiveness, and can also improve overall health and well-being.

Use gestures effectively: Using gestures in a confident and natural manner can help to convey information and express emotions in a clear and effective way.

Improving non-verbal communication, or body language, is an important aspect of effective communication. By using techniques such as observing others, practicing active listening, being aware of one's own body language, practicing good posture, and using gestures effectively, individuals can improve their non-verbal communication skills and enhance the clarity and effectiveness of their message.

Verbal Communication:

Verbal communication refers to the use of spoken words to exchange information, express thoughts and emotions, and build relationships. It is one of the most commonly used forms of communication and can be done in a variety of settings, such as face-to-face conversations, phone calls, or online chats.

Effective verbal communication requires clear and concise language, active listening, and an understanding of the nuances of language, such as tone and body language. Good verbal communication skills can help individuals to build strong relationships, convey their thoughts and emotions effectively, and achieve their goals, both in personal and professional settings.

In this section, we will explore various aspects of verbal communication, including the importance of clear and concise language, active listening, and the use of tone and body language to enhance the effectiveness of verbal communication.

Importance of Verbal Communication

The importance of verbal communication cannot be overstated. It is one of the most fundamental and widely used forms of communication and plays a crucial role in building and maintaining relationships, exchanging information, and achieving goals, both in personal and professional settings.

Verbal communication allows individuals to express their thoughts and emotions clearly and effectively, and to receive feedback and clarification in return. It is also an important tool for conflict resolution, problem-solving, and negotiation.

Effective verbal communication skills can also have a positive impact on one's personal and professional life. For example, good communication skills can help individuals to establish and maintain strong relationships, to advance in their careers, and to be more effective in achieving their goals.

In conclusion, verbal communication is an essential aspect of human interaction, and developing good verbal communication skills is a key factor in success in both personal and professional settings.

Types of Verbal Communication

There are several types of verbal communication, each with its own unique characteristics and purposes. Some of the most common types of verbal communication are:

Face-to-Face Communication: This type of communication involves a direct interaction between two or more people, either in person or via video conference. Face-to-face communication allows for the exchange of information, expressions of emotion, and the use of body language, making it one of the richest forms of communication.

Phone Calls: This type of communication involves the use of telephones to exchange information and express thoughts and emotions. Phone calls are a convenient and accessible form of communication that allows individuals to stay connected, even when they are not in the same location.

Online Chats: This type of communication involves the use of digital platforms, such as instant messaging apps or online forums, to exchange information and express thoughts and emotions. Online chats are a fast and convenient form of communication, but can also be impersonal and lack the nonverbal cues that are present in face-to-face communication.

Public Speaking: This type of communication involves the use of spoken words to present information to a large audience. Public speaking requires good verbal communication skills, as well as the ability to engage and captivate an audience.

Group Discussions: This type of communication involves a group of people exchanging ideas and opinions on a particular topic. Group discussions can be formal or informal, and are an important tool for generating new ideas, solving problems, and making decisions.

Each type of verbal communication has its own strengths and weaknesses, and it is important to choose the most appropriate form of communication based on the context and the information being exchanged.

Techniques for Improving Verbal Communication

Improving verbal communication skills is essential for success in both personal and professional settings. Here are some techniques for improving verbal communication:

Listen actively: Good communication involves not only speaking effectively, but also listening actively. Make an effort to truly understand what the other person is saying, and ask clarifying questions when necessary.

Use clear, concise language: Avoid using complex or technical language that the other person may not understand. Instead, use simple, clear, and concise language that is easy to understand.

Be assertive: Be confident and assertive in your communication, but also be respectful of others. Speak clearly and directly, and avoid using passive or vague language.

Avoid distractions: Remove any distractions, such as your phone or computer, that may take your attention away from the conversation. Give the other person your full attention and focus on what they are saying.

Nonverbal communication: Nonverbal cues, such as facial expressions, gestures, and body language, play a big role in communication. Make an effort to be aware of your own nonverbal cues, and also pay attention to the nonverbal cues of the other person.

Practice, practice, practice: Improving your verbal communication skills requires practice. Try to engage in conversations as often as possible, and seek feedback from others on your communication style.

Effective verbal communication is essential for building and maintaining relationships, exchanging information, and achieving goals. By using these techniques and continuously practicing and refining your skills, you can improve your verbal communication and become more effective in your personal and professional life.

Physical Communication

Physical communication refers to the use of physical touch and space to convey messages in a nonverbal manner. This form of communication is particularly important in personal relationships, but also has a role in professional settings, such as in healthcare or law enforcement.

Importance of Physical Communication:

Physical communication is an important aspect of human interaction, as it can convey a wide range of emotions and messages in a nonverbal manner. Physical communication can be used to express affection and support, establish power dynamics, and convey a person's emotions and thoughts.

In personal relationships, physical communication can help to strengthen bonds and convey feelings of love, comfort, and support. For example, a hug, a pat on the back, or a handshake can convey a sense of closeness and support. Physical communication can also be used to establish personal boundaries and respect for individual space and privacy.

In professional settings, physical communication can play a role in healthcare, law enforcement, and other fields where it is important to convey a sense of authority and control. A confident handshake or a strong, assertive posture can convey a sense of confidence and leadership, while a gentle touch or comforting gesture can convey compassion and support.

Therefore, physical communication is an important tool for building and maintaining relationships, conveying emotions and thoughts, and achieving goals in both personal and professional settings. It is crucial to be mindful of your own physical communication and to understand how it may be perceived by others.

Types of Physical Communication:

Physical communication encompasses a wide range of nonverbal behaviors, including gestures, posture, facial expressions, and touch. Some common types of physical communication include:

Gestures: These are movements of the hands, arms, and body that can convey a wide range of meanings and emotions. Common gestures include pointing, waving, shrugging, and nodding.

Posture: A person's posture can convey a great deal about their mood, emotions, and confidence. For example, a person who is slouching may be seen as lacking confidence, while a person who is standing tall and confident may be perceived as assertive and in control.

Facial Expressions: Facial expressions are an important aspect of nonverbal communication, as they can convey a wide range of emotions, from happiness and excitement to sadness and anger.

Touch: Touch can convey a wide range of emotions, from affection and comfort to aggression and anger. It is also an important aspect of physical communication in professional settings, such as in healthcare, where touch can convey a sense of compassion and support.

These are just a few examples of the types of physical communication that people use on a daily basis. Understanding the different types of physical communication and how they can be used effectively can help you to improve your own communication skills and build stronger relationships.

Techniques for Improving Physical Communication

Improving physical communication can help you to build stronger relationships, convey emotions and thoughts more effectively, and achieve your goals in both personal and professional settings. Here are a few techniques for improving physical communication:

Pay attention to your body language: Be mindful of your own physical communication and pay attention to how it may be perceived by others. Practice good posture, make eye contact, and use gestures and facial expressions that convey your intended message.

Watch others: Observe the physical communication of others and consider how it affects your perception of them. This can help you to identify the types of physical communication that are most effective and to incorporate these techniques into your own communication style.

Practice active listening: When communicating with others, make an effort to be present and engaged in the conversation. Pay attention to their physical cues and respond appropriately, using gestures, posture, and facial expressions to convey empathy and understanding.

Use touch appropriately: Touch can be a powerful tool for conveying emotions, but it is important to use it appropriately. Respect personal boundaries and be mindful of the cultural norms and expectations that may affect the use of touch in different settings.

Seek feedback: Ask others for feedback on your physical communication and consider their observations and suggestions for improvement.

By incorporating these techniques into your communication style, you can improve your physical communication skills and build stronger relationships with the people around you.

Recap of Key Points

In conclusion, effective communication is essential for building and maintaining relationships, exchanging information, and achieving goals. Communication can take many forms, including face-to-face, verbal, and physical communication.

In face-to-face communication, tone of voice, body language (non-verbal communication), and other physical cues play a critical role in conveying meaning and emotions. Improving your tone of voice, non-verbal communication, and physical communication skills can help you to build stronger relationships, express your thoughts and emotions more effectively, and achieve your goals.

Verbal communication is also important for exchanging information and building relationships. Improving your verbal communication skills can involve paying attention to your language, listening actively, and seeking feedback from others.

Finally, physical communication plays a critical role in conveying emotions and establishing connections with others. Improving your physical communication skills may involve paying attention to your body language, observing others, practicing active listening, using touch appropriately, and seeking feedback.

By developing and refining these various forms of communication, you can build stronger relationships, exchange information more effectively, and achieve your goals in both personal and professional settings.

The Importance of Effective Communication

Effective communication is crucial for success in all aspects of life, both personal and professional. The ability to communicate effectively can impact everything from relationships and personal interactions to success in the workplace and achieving goals. Some of the key benefits of effective communication include:

Building Relationships: Effective communication is the foundation of strong and healthy relationships, allowing individuals to understand and be understood, express their thoughts and emotions, and build trust and rapport.

Exchanging Information: Communication allows individuals to exchange information and ideas, and to share knowledge and experience. This is especially important in the workplace, where clear and effective communication is necessary for teams to work together effectively and achieve their goals.

Making Decisions: Effective communication allows individuals to make informed decisions by gathering and processing information from others. Whether in personal or professional settings, good communication skills enable individuals to make informed and confident choices.

Resolving Conflicts: Communication is also essential for resolving conflicts and misunderstandings, as it allows individuals to express their opinions and concerns, listen to others, and find mutually acceptable solutions.

Effective communication is vital for success in all aspects of life. By developing and refining your communication skills, you can build stronger relationships, exchange information more effectively, make informed decisions, and resolve conflicts more effectively.

effective communication is a critical skill that can have a profound impact on all aspects of life. By understanding the different forms of communication, including face-to-face communication, tone of voice, body language, verbal communication, and physical communication, you can improve your overall communication skills.

Some final thoughts and recommendations for improving your communication skills

include:

Practice active listening: Pay close attention to the person you are communicating with and show that you are listening by making eye contact, nodding, and asking questions.

Be aware of non-verbal cues: Your body language, gestures, and facial expressions can often convey just as much meaning as your words. Be mindful of your non-verbal cues and adjust them as necessary to match your tone and message.

Speak clearly and confidently: When speaking, articulate your words clearly and speak at a pace that is easy for others to follow. Confidence in your words and message can help to engage others and get your message across effectively.

Be open-minded: Be open to others' perspectives and ideas, and approach communication with a willingness to learn and understand.

By following these recommendations and continually working to improve your communication skills, you can become an effective communicator and achieve success in all areas of your life.

VI

Communication Styles

Communication Styles: How They Affect Our Interactions

Effective communication is vital for any relationship, be it personal or professional. However, not everyone communicates in the same way. People have different communication styles that can affect the way they express themselves, listen to others, and build relationships. Understanding and adapting to these communication styles can enhance our interactions and prevent misunderstandings. In this essay, we will explore the different communication styles and their impact on our interactions.

An Introduction to the Communication Styles Matrix

Effective communication is key to building and maintaining strong relationships, whether in our personal or professional lives. However, different people communicate in different ways. Understanding these communication styles can help us better connect with others and avoid misunderstandings. In this essay, we will explore the Communication Styles Matrix, a tool used to identify and understand different communication styles. We will discuss each of the four styles: Direct, Spirited, Systematic, and Considerate, with examples of each.

The Communication Styles Matrix is a model used to describe how individuals communicate with others. It is based on two dimensions: assertiveness and responsiveness. Assertiveness is the degree to which a person communicates their thoughts and feelings to others, while responsiveness is the degree to which they listen to and acknowledge others' thoughts and feelings. The four styles of communication that emerge from this model are Direct, Spirited, Systematic, and Considerate.

Overview of the Four Communication Styles

The first communication style in the matrix is the Direct communication style. This style is characterized by high assertiveness and low responsiveness. Individuals with a Direct communication style are often seen as confident, blunt, and straightforward. They express their thoughts and feelings clearly and are not afraid to speak their minds. They tend to focus on the task at hand rather than the people involved. An example of someone with a Direct communication style is a CEO who delivers a bold and decisive message to their employees.

The second communication style in the matrix is the Spirited communication style. This style is characterized by high assertiveness and high responsiveness. Individuals with a Spirited communication style are seen as energetic, passionate, and enthusiastic. They express their thoughts and feelings with great emotion and tend to focus on people more than the task at hand. An example of someone with a Spirited communication style is a motivational speaker who inspires and energizes their audience.

The third communication style in the matrix is the Systematic communication style. This style is characterized by low assertiveness and high responsiveness. Individuals with a Systematic communication style are often seen as analytical, detailed, and objective. They tend to express their thoughts and feelings in a logical and structured way and are good at listening to and acknowledging others. They tend to focus on the task at hand and may have a difficult time understanding the emotions of others. An example of someone with a Systematic communication style is an engineer who explains technical details to a client in a clear and concise manner.

The fourth and final communication style in the matrix is the Considerate communication style. This style is characterized by low assertiveness and low responsiveness. Individuals with a Considerate communication style are seen as polite, friendly, and accommodating. They tend to avoid conflict and may have a difficult time expressing their thoughts and feelings. They focus on building relationships and may have difficulty focusing on the task at hand. An example of someone with a Considerate communication style is a customer service representative who listens patiently to a customer's concerns and offers a solution in a friendly and understanding manner.

Understanding different communication styles is crucial to building and maintaining strong relationships. The Communication Styles Matrix is a useful tool for identifying and understanding different communication styles. The Direct, Spirited, Systematic, and Considerate communication styles are all valid and valuable ways of communicating, and each has its own strengths and weaknesses. By being aware of our own communication style and adapting it to fit the situation, we can communicate more effectively and connect with others more deeply.

The Direct Communication Style: Benefits and Challenges

Communication is an essential aspect of human interaction, and it takes many forms. One of the most straightforward styles of communication is the direct communication style. In this essay, we will explore the Direct Communication Style, a communication style that emphasizes clear and concise communication, and its benefits and challenges.

The Direct Communication Style is characterized by a clear and straightforward communication approach. Those who use this style often express their thoughts and feelings in an honest and direct manner, without the use of sugar-coating or any form of beating around the bush. People who use this style are often seen as assertive and confident, as they are not afraid to express themselves and get straight to the point. They are also seen as decisive, as they can communicate their thoughts and feelings in a way that leaves no room for ambiguity or confusion.

One of the primary benefits of the Direct Communication Style is that it is time-efficient. When people use this style, they do not waste time or beat around the bush, which can help to eliminate misunderstandings or confusion that might arise when messages are communicated indirectly. It also helps to avoid misinterpretation of the message, as it is clear and direct, leaving no room for confusion.

In addition, the Direct Communication Style can also help to establish trust and credibility. When people communicate directly, they are seen as honest, transparent, and trustworthy, which can help to establish a strong rapport with others. This style of communication is also useful in high-stress situations where decisions need to be made quickly, as it allows for a quick and decisive response.

However, the Direct Communication Style can also present some challenges. For example, when used inappropriately, it can come across as rude, abrasive, or confrontational. It can also be challenging to use this style with people who are more sensitive, as it can come across as aggressive or intimidating. Additionally, the direct communication style may not be suitable for situations that require a more diplomatic approach.

The Direct Communication Style can be a powerful tool in establishing credibility, trust, and efficient communication. By being direct and clear in their communication, individuals can save time, avoid misunderstandings, and establish strong relationships. However, it is essential to be mindful of the audience and the situation, as inappropriate use of the Direct Communication Style can lead to negative consequences. By balancing the benefits and challenges of this style, individuals can use it to their advantage in both personal and professional settings.

The Spirited Communication Style: Harnessing the Power of Passion

"Expressiveness adds excitement to life's moments and strengthens bonds between friends."

Effective communication is an essential aspect of our daily lives, and it takes many forms. One of the most dynamic styles of communication is the Spirited Communication Style. In this essay, we will explore the Spirited Communication Style, a communication style that emphasizes the use of passion, energy, and enthusiasm to convey ideas and opinions.

The Spirited Communication Style is characterized by an emphasis on energy, enthusiasm, and passion in communication. Those who use this style often express themselves with great enthusiasm, using gestures, voice modulation, and facial expressions to convey their message. People who use this style are often seen as energetic, passionate, and engaging, as they can inspire and motivate others through their communication style.

One of the primary benefits of the Spirited Communication Style is that it can be incredibly motivating. When people use this style, they are more likely to engage and inspire their audience, as they convey their message with great passion and enthusiasm. This style of communication can be particularly effective in situations where individuals need to motivate others or generate excitement around a particular topic or idea.

In addition, the Spirited Communication Style can also help individuals to build strong relationships with others. When people communicate with passion and enthusiasm, they can create a sense of connection and shared excitement that can help to establish strong relationships with others. This can be particularly useful in a professional context, where the ability to build relationships can be critical to success.

However, the Spirited Communication Style can also present some challenges. For example, individuals who use this style may come across as too intense or overwhelming, which can be off-putting for some people. Additionally, this style of communication may not be suitable for situations that require a more serious or subdued tone.

The Spirited Communication Style can be a powerful tool for individuals who want to inspire and motivate others through their communication. By using energy, enthusiasm, and passion, individuals can create a sense of connection and excitement that can help to build strong relationships and inspire others. However, it is essential to be mindful of the audience and the situation, as inappropriate use of the Spirited Communication Style can lead to negative consequences. By balancing the benefits and challenges of this style, individuals can use it to their advantage in both personal and professional settings.

"Bringing excitement and energy to the table, this young businessman is ready to tackle any challenge with his spirited communication style."

The Systematic Communication Style: The Power of Precision

Communication is a fundamental aspect of human interaction, and the way we communicate can impact the effectiveness of our interactions. The Systematic Communication Style is one of the communication styles that prioritizes precision, clarity, and structure. In this essay, we will explore the Systematic Communication Style, its characteristics, benefits, and challenges.

The Systematic Communication Style is characterized by a preference for precision, clarity, and structure in communication. Individuals who use this style prioritize the organization of their thoughts and the presentation of their ideas in a clear and logical manner. They may also be inclined to use data, facts, and evidence to support their arguments.

One of the primary benefits of the Systematic Communication Style is that it can be incredibly effective in situations that require clarity and precision. This style of communication can be particularly useful in professional contexts where individuals need to convey complex information, instructions, or procedures. The Systematic Communication Style can help ensure that the information is presented in a clear and concise manner, reducing the likelihood of confusion or misinterpretation.

Moreover, the Systematic Communication Style can also facilitate critical thinking and decision-making. This style of communication involves a systematic approach to problem-solving and decision-making, which can help individuals to identify and evaluate all relevant factors before making a decision. This style is particularly useful in situations that require analytical thinking, such as scientific research, engineering, or financial analysis.

However, the Systematic Communication Style can also present some challenges. For example, individuals who use this style may come across as too rigid or inflexible, which can be off-putting for some people. Moreover, this style of communication may not be suitable for situations that require a more personal or emotional tone, such as interpersonal relationships or creative endeavors.

The Systematic Communication Style can be a powerful tool for individuals who value clarity, precision, and structure in their communication. This style can be particularly useful in professional contexts where the effective communication of complex information is critical. By prioritizing clarity and precision in their communication, individuals can facilitate critical thinking and decision-making. However, it is essential to be mindful of the audience and the situation, as inappropriate use of the Systematic

Communication Style can lead to negative consequences. By balancing the benefits and challenges of this style, individuals can use it to their advantage in both personal and professional settings.

The Considerate Communication Style: The Power of Empathy

Effective communication is critical to building and maintaining healthy relationships. The Considerate Communication Style is one of the communication styles that prioritize empathy, understanding, and respect. In this essay, we will explore the Considerate Communication Style, its characteristics, benefits, and challenges.

The Considerate Communication Style is characterized by a preference for empathy, understanding, and respect in communication. Individuals who use this style prioritize the needs and feelings of the other person and take great care to ensure that their message is delivered in a way that is sensitive and considerate. They may also be inclined to use active listening skills and to seek clarification to ensure that they understand the other person's perspective.

One of the primary benefits of the Considerate Communication Style is that it can be incredibly effective in building and maintaining healthy relationships. This style of communication can help individuals to build trust, foster a sense of safety and security, and promote open and honest communication. The Considerate Communication Style can be particularly useful in personal relationships, such as friendships, romantic partnerships, and family relationships.

Moreover, the Considerate Communication Style can also facilitate conflict resolution and problem-solving. This style of communication involves a willingness to listen to and consider the other person's perspective, which can help individuals to identify and understand the root causes of the conflict or problem. This style is particularly useful in situations that require negotiation, compromise, and collaboration.

However, the Considerate Communication Style can also present some challenges. For example, individuals who use this style may struggle to assert their needs and boundaries, which can lead to feelings of frustration or resentment. Moreover, this style of communication may not be suitable for situations that require a more direct or assertive approach, such as in business negotiations or legal proceedings.

The Considerate Communication Style can be a powerful tool for individuals who value empathy, understanding, and respect in their communication. This style can be particularly useful in personal relationships where building and maintaining trust is critical. By prioritizing empathy and active listening in their communication, individuals can facilitate conflict resolution and problem-solving. However, it is essential to be mindful of the audience and the situation, as inappropriate use of the Considerate Communication Style can lead to negative consequences. By balancing the benefits and challenges of this style, individuals can use it to their advantage in both personal and professional settings.

VII

Basic Listening Skills

"Empathy and understanding: The key to effective
communication through active listening

As English speakers, it is crucial that we develop and refine our
listening skills. But what exactly do we mean by "listening skills"?
Listening skills refer to our ability to comprehend, interpret, and

respond to spoken language effectively. In other words, listening skills are the foundation of effective communication.

The importance of basic listening skills cannot be overstated. Good listeners are able to establish better relationships, make more informed decisions, and solve problems more effectively than those who struggle with listening. In the workplace, effective listening is a key factor in job success, as it enables employees to understand instructions, collaborate with colleagues, and participate in meetings and presentations.

Listening is a critical component of communication, yet it is often overlooked and undervalued. It is the process of receiving and interpreting messages from another person, whether it is spoken or unspoken. Listening is a complex and active process that requires focus, attention, and effort.

Definition of Listening

Listening is more than just hearing the words spoken by another person. It is the process of actively engaging with the speaker, paying attention to their words, tone, and body language, and attempting to understand the message they are trying to convey. Listening requires concentration, patience, and the ability to put aside one's own thoughts and biases. Effective listening involves both hearing the words spoken and comprehending the intended message.

Different Types of Listening

Listening is a complex process that can take on different forms depending on the context and the listener's goals. In this chapter, we will explore six different types of listening: superficial listening, appreciative listening, focused listening, evaluative listening, empathic listening, and critical listening.

A. Superficial Listening

Superficial listening is a type of listening that occurs when the listener is only paying attention to the surface level of the message, without making an effort to understand the deeper meaning. This type of listening is often characterized by inattentiveness, lack of engagement, and a lack of effort to understand the message.

B. Appreciative Listening

Appreciative listening is a type of listening that is focused on enjoying and appreciating the message, rather than critically evaluating it. This type of listening is often used when listening to music, art, or other forms of entertainment. The listener is not focused on understanding the message in detail, but rather on experiencing and enjoying the message.

C. Focused Listening

Focused listening is a type of listening that is focused on understanding the message in detail. This type of listening is often used in educational or professional settings, where the listener needs to understand the message in order to make informed decisions or solve problems. Focused listening requires paying attention to the message, taking notes, and asking questions to clarify information.

D. Evaluative Listening

Evaluative listening is a type of listening that involves evaluating the message, either positively or negatively. This type of listening is often used in professional settings, where the listener needs to make a judgement about the message in order to make informed decisions. Evaluative listening requires paying attention to the message, critically evaluating the information, and making a judgement about the message.

E. Empathic Listening

Empathic listening is a type of listening that is focused on understanding the speaker's perspective and feelings. This type of listening requires paying attention to the speaker's words, tone, and body language, and trying to understand their perspective and feelings. Empathic listening is often used in personal or therapeutic relationships, where the listener needs to understand the speaker's perspective and feelings in order to provide support and understanding.

F. Critical Listening

Critical listening is a type of listening that involves evaluating the message and the speaker's arguments. This type of listening requires paying attention to the message, critically evaluating the information, and making a judgement about the arguments presented. Critical listening is often used in professional and academic settings, where the listener needs to make informed decisions and evaluate the quality of the arguments presented.

In conclusion, different types of listening are used in different contexts and for different purposes. Understanding the different types of listening can help you to become a more effective listener, by allowing you to choose the type of listening that is appropriate for each situation.

Importance of Listening in Communication

Listening plays a crucial role in communication. It enables individuals to build rapport, establish trust, and deepen relationships. When people listen to each other, they are able to understand each other's perspectives, thoughts, and feelings. This fosters mutual respect and helps to resolve conflicts and misunderstandings.

In the workplace, effective listening is essential for teamwork, productivity, and success. When team members listen to each other, they are able to exchange ideas, collaborate on projects, and make decisions more effectively. Good listeners also tend to be better leaders, as they are able to understand the needs and perspectives of their team members.

Active listening

Active listening is a technique of paying close attention to the speaker in order to fully understand their message. It involves not only hearing the words being spoken, but also being aware of the speaker's tone, body language, and nonverbal cues.

To be an effective active listener, it is important to:

1. Focus your attention on the speaker. Avoid distractions such as looking at your phone or daydreaming.
2. Ask clarifying questions. If you are unsure about something the speaker has said, ask for clarification.
3. Paraphrase. Repeat what the speaker has said in your own words to show that you are paying attention and to confirm your understanding.
4. Provide feedback. Let the speaker know that you are paying attention by nodding, making eye contact, and providing verbal affirmations such as "I see" or "I understand".

By using these active listening techniques, you will be able to better understand the speaker's message and respond in a more meaningful way. Active listening is an essential technique in effective communication and is the practice of paying full attention to the speaker, not just physically but also mentally and emotionally. It involves not just hearing the words but also understanding the context and emotions behind those words.

For example, if a friend is telling you about a marriage breakup, active listening would involve making eye contact, asking clarifying questions, and being empathetic and supportive. This shows the speaker that you are fully engaged in the conversation and helps to build trust and deepen the relationship.

Active listening can also be useful in professional settings, such as in a meeting with colleagues or a performance review with a manager. In these situations, it's important to listen carefully to understand the speaker's perspectives, goals, and needs. This can help you to respond in a way that is more aligned with the speaker's intentions, leading to more productive and positive outcomes.

To practice active listening, try the following techniques:

1. Make eye contact with the speaker
2. Avoid distractions such as checking your phone or multitasking
3. Repeat what the speaker has said to show that you are paying attention
4. Ask clarifying questions to make sure you understand
5. Show empathy and support by using verbal and nonverbal cues

By using active listening techniques, you can improve your communication skills, build better relationships, and achieve more positive outcomes in your personal and professional life.

Active vs. Passive Listening

Listening can take on many forms, but it is generally classified as either active or passive. Understanding the differences between these two forms of listening and the advantages of active listening is crucial for effective communication.

A. Differences between Active and Passive Listening

Passive listening involves simply hearing the words spoken by the speaker without actively engaging with the message. This type of listening often occurs when the listener is distracted, disinterested, or lacks attention and focus. Passive listeners may nod their head or say "uh-huh" to acknowledge the speaker, but they are not fully present in the moment and may not retain much of the information conveyed.

Active listening, on the other hand, involves actively engaging with the speaker, paying attention to their words, tone, and body language, and attempting to understand the message they are trying to convey. Active listeners provide verbal and non-verbal cues to indicate they are listening, ask questions, and paraphrase what they have heard to confirm their understanding.

B. *Advantages of Active Listening*

Active listening offers several advantages over passive listening. When people listen actively, they are able to understand the message being conveyed more thoroughly and retain the information more effectively. Active listening also enhances relationships and helps to resolve conflicts, as it demonstrates that the listener cares about the speaker's perspective and is invested in understanding their point of view.

In the workplace, active listening can improve teamwork, increase productivity, and foster a positive work environment. When team members listen actively to each other, they are able to exchange ideas, collaborate on projects, and make decisions more effectively.

C. *Common Mistakes in Passive Listening*

Passive listening can lead to several mistakes, including misunderstandings, conflicts, and missed opportunities. When listeners are passive, they may not retain important information, leading to confusion and frustration. They may also miss out on opportunities to contribute to the conversation or offer suggestions and ideas.

Passive listening can also cause harm to relationships, as it can make the speaker feel ignored or unvalued. When people feel like they are not being listened to, they may become frustrated, resentful, or disengaged, which can lead to conflicts and breakdowns in communication.

While passive listening may seem like a more passive approach, it can lead to several mistakes and have negative consequences. By contrast, active listening is a proactive and effective approach to communication that can greatly improve relationships, enhance understanding, and lead to more positive outcomes.

Self Awareness

Self-awareness is the first step in becoming a better listener.Self awareness is a critical component of effective listening. Understanding one's own listening habits, biases, and filters can help individuals become better listeners and improve their communication skills.

Understanding Your Listening Habits

To become a better listener, it is important to understand your own listening habits. Are you a passive listener or an active listener? Do you get distracted easily or find it difficult to concentrate? By identifying your strengths and weaknesses as a listener, you can work to improve your listening skills and become more effective in your communication.

Identifying Your Biases and Filters

Everyone has biases and filters that can impact their ability to listen effectively. These biases can come in many forms, including cultural, personal, and situational. By becoming aware of your biases, you can work to overcome them and become a more effective listener.

Developing Self Awareness for Effective Listening

Developing self awareness for effective listening requires a willingness to reflect on your own listening habits and biases. This can be achieved through self-reflection, seeking feedback from others, and seeking out training and resources to help improve your listening skills.

Additionally, practicing active listening can help improve self awareness. When you engage in active listening, you become more aware of your own thoughts and reactions to what is being said.

This can help you identify areas for improvement and work to overcome any biases or filters that may be impacting your listening skills.

Becoming an Active Listener

Becoming an active listener is a process that requires effort and commitment, but it can greatly improve communication and relationships. In this chapter, we will explore the key components of active listening, the steps involved in the process of active listening, and techniques for improving active listening skills.

A. Key Components of Active Listening

Active listening involves several key components, including paying attention, showing empathy, and providing feedback. It also requires being present in the moment and fully engaged in the conversation. Active listeners pay attention to the speaker's words, tone, and body language, and try to understand the message they are trying to convey. They also show empathy by trying to understand the speaker's perspective and feeling their emotions. Finally, active listeners provide feedback to the speaker by acknowledging what they have heard and offering clarification or paraphrasing to confirm their understanding.

B. Steps Involved in the Process of Active Listening

The process of active listening involves several steps:

Pay attention to the speaker: This involves focusing on the speaker and minimizing distractions.

Show empathy: Try to understand the speaker's perspective and feelings.

Provide feedback: Offer verbal or non-verbal cues to acknowledge what you have heard and provide clarification or paraphrasing to confirm your understanding.

Ask questions: Ask open-ended questions to encourage the speaker to elaborate on their thoughts and feelings.

Reflect: Take a moment to reflect on what you have heard and what you have learned.

C. Techniques for Improving Active Listening Skills

To become a better active listener, it is important to practice the steps involved in the process of active listening. Some techniques for improving active listening skills include:

Eliminating distractions: Turn off your phone, close your computer, and minimize other distractions to focus on the conversation.

Practice empathy: Try to put yourself in the speaker's shoes and understand their perspective and feelings.

Provide feedback: Offer verbal or non-verbal cues to acknowledge what you have heard and provide clarification or paraphrasing to confirm your understanding.

Ask questions: Ask open-ended questions to encourage the speaker to elaborate on their thoughts and feelings.

Reflect: Take a moment to reflect on what you have heard and what you have learned.

In conclusion, becoming an active listener is a process that requires effort and commitment. By understanding the key components of active listening, the steps involved in the process, and techniques for improving active listening skills, you can become a better listener and improve your communication skills.

Reasons for Poor Listening

Poor listening habits can have a significant impact on communication and can lead to misunderstandings, frustration, and poor decision making. In this chapter, we will explore the common causes of poor listening and the impact it can have on communication. We will also discuss strategies for overcoming poor listening habits.

A. *Common Causes of Poor Listening*

There are many factors that can contribute to poor listening, including:

Distractions: Distractions, such as background noise or other stimuli, can interfere with your ability to listen effectively.

Speed of Thought: Our thoughts can often race ahead of what is being said, making it difficult to stay focused on the message.

Preconceptions: Our preconceived notions and biases can affect our ability to listen objectively and without judgement.

Multitasking: Multitasking, or trying to do multiple things at once, can also impact our ability to listen effectively.

Poor Listening Habits: Over time, poor listening habits can become deeply ingrained, making it difficult to change our behavior and improve our listening skills.

B. *Impact of Poor Listening on Communication*

Poor listening can have a negative impact on communication, leading to misunderstandings, miscommunication, and conflict. It can also lead to poor decision making, as you may not have all the information you need to make an informed decision.

C. *How to Overcome Poor Listening Habits*

To overcome poor listening habits, it is important to become more self-aware of your listening habits and to work on developing active listening skills. Some strategies for overcoming poor listening habits include:

Paying Attention: Make an effort to focus on the speaker and the message, rather than letting your thoughts wander.

Avoiding Distractions: Find a quiet, distraction-free environment to listen in, and eliminate distractions where possible.

Practicing Active Listening: Develop active listening skills by asking questions, repeating back what you have heard, and making an effort to understand the message and the speaker's perspective.

Challenging Your Biases: Be aware of your preconceptions and biases, and work on letting go of them when you are listening to others.

Focusing on One Task at a Time: Avoid multitasking, as it can interfere with your ability to listen effectively.

By following these strategies, you can overcome poor listening habits and become a more effective listener.

Barriers to Effective Listening

Effective listening is a critical component of successful communication, but there are many barriers that can get in the way. In this chapter, we will explore some of the common barriers to effective listening and discuss strategies for overcoming them.

Common Barriers to Effective Listening

Some of the common barriers to effective listening include:

Distractions: Distractions, such as background noise or other stimuli, can interfere with your ability to listen effectively.

Speed of Thought: Our thoughts can often race ahead of what is being said, making it difficult to stay focused on the message.

Preconceptions: Our preconceived notions and biases can affect our ability to listen objectively and without judgement.

Multitasking: Multitasking, or trying to do multiple things at once, can also impact our ability to listen effectively.Emotional Reactions: Strong emotional reactions can also interfere with our ability to listen effectively, as they can cause us to focus on our own thoughts andB. How Barriers Affect Communication

feelings rather than on the message being conveyed.

How Barriers Affect Communication

Barriers to effective listening can have a negative impact on communication, leading to misunderstandings, miscommunication, and conflict. They can also lead to poor decision making, as you may not have all the information you need to make an informed decision.

Techniques for Overcoming Barriers to Effective Listening

To overcome barriers to effective listening, it is important to become more self-aware of your listening habits and to work on developing active listening skills. Some strategies for overcoming barriers to effective listening include:

Paying Attention: Make an effort to focus on the speaker and the message, rather than letting your thoughts wander.

Avoiding Distractions: Find a quiet, distraction-free environment to listen in, and eliminate distractions where possible.

Practicing Active Listening: Develop active listening skills by asking questions, repeating back what you have heard, and making an effort to understand the message and the speaker's perspective.

Challenging Your Biases: Be aware of your preconceptions and biases, and work on letting go of them when you are listening to others.

Focusing on One Task at a Time: Avoid multitasking, as it can interfere with your ability to listen effectively.

Managing Emotions: If you find yourself becoming emotional, take a moment to process your feelings and return to the task of listening.

Importance of Awareness and Mindfulness in Identifying and Overcoming Barriers

Awareness and mindfulness are critical in identifying and overcoming barriers to effective listening. By being aware of your own thoughts, feelings, and habits, you can identify the barriers that are getting in the way of effective listening and develop strategies for overcoming them.

By becoming more aware and mindful of the barriers to effective listening, and by working on developing active listening skills, you can overcome these barriers and become a more effective listener.

Listening in Difficult Situations

In some situations, effective listening can be especially challenging.

A. Understanding the Challenges of Listening in Difficult Situations

Difficult situations can arise in any type of communication and can include disagreements, confrontations, or emotionally charged conversations. Listening effectively in these situations requires a high level of self-awareness, empathy, and active listening skills.

B. Techniques for Effective Listening in Challenging Conversations

In order to listen effectively in difficult situations, it is important to:

Remain calm and neutral: Maintaining a calm demeanor and avoiding reacting emotionally can help you stay focused on the message being conveyed.

Practice empathy: Empathy is the ability to understand and share the feelings of others. By practicing empathy, you can better understand the perspectives of others and respond in a way that is respectful and supportive.

Focus on understanding: Rather than focusing on responding or defending yourself, focus on understanding the other person's perspective. Ask clarifying questions and repeat back what you have heard to ensure you have accurately understood the message.

Examples of Difficult Situations and How to Listen Effectively

Some examples of difficult situations include:

Disagreements: When there is a disagreement, it is important to listen to the other person's perspective and respond in a way that is respectful and non-combative.

Confrontations: In confrontational situations, it is important to remain calm and avoid reacting emotionally. Practice active listening skills and focus on understanding the other person's perspective.

Emotionally charged conversations: When emotions are running high, it is important to remain calm and practice empathy. Listen carefully to the other person's words and respond in a way that is respectful and supportive.

Importance of Empathy and Active Listening in Difficult Situations

In difficult situations, the ability to listen effectively can have a major impact on the outcome of the conversation. By practicing empathy and active listening, you can improve your ability to understand the perspectives of others and respond in a way that is respectful and supportive.

Here are a few tips to become a better listener in difficult situations:

1. Maintain a calm demeanor: In challenging situations, it is important to stay calm and composed. This can help the speaker feel heard and respected, and increase the chances of a productive conversation.
2. Show empathy: Put yourself in the speaker's shoes and try to understand their perspective. By showing empathy, you can help the speaker feel heard and validated.

3. Avoid interrupting: Let the speaker speak without interrupting. This can help avoid misunderstandings and ensure that the speaker feels heard.

4. Ask clarifying questions: If you are unsure about something the speaker has said, ask clarifying questions. This can help you better understand the speaker's perspective and avoid misinterpretations.

5. Be non-judgmental: Avoid making assumptions or being judgmental. Instead, listen with an open mind and strive to understand the speaker's point of view.

Example 1: Imagine you are in a coffee shop and a close friend of yours, Pavani, comes to meet you to share her problems. She has been going through a tough time lately and wants to talk to you about it.

As a good active listener, you focus your attention on Pavani. You put your phone away and make sure to give her your undivided attention. You avoid any distractions and show her that you are fully present in the moment.

As Pavani starts talking, you realize that you are not fully understanding what she is trying to say. So, you ask clarifying questions to get a better understanding of the situation. You ask, "Can you explain that in more detail?" and "What do you mean by that?" to make sure you have a clear understanding of what she is going through.

To show that you are truly paying attention, you paraphrase what Pavani has said. You repeat her words in your own words and say, "So, what you're trying to say is that you're feeling overwhelmed and don't know how to handle everything?" This confirms your understanding and lets Pavani know that you are truly listening.

As Pavani continues to talk, you provide her with feedback by nodding your head, making eye contact, and giving verbal affirmations such as "I understand" and "That must have been really difficult for you." These gestures let Maria know that you are paying attention and empathize with her situation.

In this scenario, you have demonstrated the important elements of active listening: focusing your attention, asking clarifying questions, paraphrasing, and providing feedback. By doing so, you have shown Pavani that you are truly there for her and that you care about what she has to say.

Example 2: Imagine you are in a meeting with a coworker who is presenting a new project idea. As an active listener, you are focused solely on the speaker and are determined to truly understand the project.

You notice that there are some aspects of the project that you don't quite understand, so you ask clarifying questions. "Can you explain more about the budget for this project?" you ask.

Your coworker explains the budget in further detail, and to ensure you understand, you paraphrase what they have said. "So, I understand that the budget for this project is Rs 50,0000 and it will be spread out over the next 6 months," you say.

As your coworker continues to present their idea, you nod, make eye contact, and provide verbal affirmations like "I see" and "That makes sense". This lets the speaker know that you are engaged and interested in what they have to say.

By being an active listener and utilizing these techniques, you can ensure that you have a clear understanding of the project and are able to provide valuable feedback and insights.

Example 3: Imagine you're in a job interview for your dream position. The interviewer is asking you a question and you're eager to answer, but you're so focused on what you want to say next that you don't really hear what they're asking. You blurt out a response that doesn't really answer their question, and you can tell from the look on their face that you've missed the mark.

Now, imagine the same situation, but this time you're a good listener. You're focused on the interviewer and what they're asking, and you ask clarifying questions to make sure you understand. You provide feedback by nodding and making eye contact, showing the interviewer that you're engaged and interested. When you respond, you answer the question directly and effectively, impressing the interviewer with your communication skills.

This scenario shows the difference between someone who struggles with listening and someone who has mastered basic listening skills. By paying attention, asking questions, and providing feedback, you can demonstrate that you're a strong communicator and a valuable asset in any situation.

In a social setting, good listening skills can also greatly enhance relationships. By truly paying attention and actively listening to others, individuals can deepen their connections and build stronger bonds with their friends and family. Moreover, effective listening allows people to better understand others' perspectives, resolve conflicts, and provide emotional support.

Example 4

Imagine you are at a restaurant with a group of friends, and one of them is telling a story that is important to them. Your phone vibrates with a text message, and your initial reaction is to check it. But you remember the importance of handling distractions and put your phone away, focusing all of your attention on your friend.

As they continue speaking, they become emotional and upset. You can see that they are struggling to express themselves. In this moment, it is crucial to deal with emotional speakers. You take a deep breath and try to understand their perspective, remaining calm and empathetic. You listen to understand their message, avoiding any urge to interrupt or dismiss their feelings.

You try to practice empathy by putting yourself in their shoes and imagining what they might be feeling. This helps you understand their message more deeply, and respond in a way that is supportive and meaningful.

By handling distractions, dealing with emotional speakers, listening to understand, and practicing empathy, you are demonstrating excellent basic listening skills and making a positive impact on the conversation.

Listening Training

Developing and improving your listening skills requires intentional effort and practice. In this chapter, we will discuss the benefits of listening training and offer techniques and resources for improving your listening skills.

Benefits of Listening Training

Improved Communication: By improving your listening skills, you can communicate more effectively with others and reduce misunderstandings.

Better Relationships: Listening training can help you build stronger relationships by showing others that you value their thoughts and opinions.

Increased Confidence: Improved listening skills can increase your confidence in communication situations, making it easier for you to express yourself effectively.

Career Advancement: Effective listening is an important skill in the workplace, and can lead to increased opportunities for career advancement.

Techniques for Improving Listening Skills

Practice Active Listening: Active listening requires focus and effort, and the more you practice, the better you will become at it.

Seek Feedback: Ask friends, family, and coworkers for feedback on your listening skills, and use their feedback to identify areas for improvement.

Focus on Understanding: Rather than focusing on responding or defending yourself, focus on understanding the other person's perspective.

Stay Open Minded: Avoid making assumptions and stay open to different perspectives, even if you don't agree with them.

Resources for Listening Training

Books and Articles: There are many books and articles available that offer tips and techniques for improving your listening skills.

Workshops and Courses: Workshops and courses on active listening and effective communication can provide hands-on training and opportunities for practice.

Online Videos: There are many online videos and tutorials available that offer tips and techniques for improving your listening skills.

By incorporating these techniques and resources into your listening training, you can improve your ability to listen effectively and communicate more successfully with others.

Case Studies

The Story of a Salesperson and an Active Listener

Sarika was a successful salesperson, known for her exceptional communication skills. She was always eager to understand the needs and concerns of her clients, and she would do everything in her power to provide them with the best solutions. One day, she met a new client named James, who was looking to purchase a new software system for his business.

At first, James was skeptical of Sarika's approach, as he had been burned by salespeople in the past who made promises they couldn't keep. But as Sarika began to ask questions and listen actively to his concerns, James realized that she was different. She was genuinely interested in understanding his needs, and she was determined to find a solution that would work for him.

Sarika's active listening skills allowed her to gain a deep understanding of James's needs, and she was able to recommend a software system that was tailored to his specific requirements. James was impressed by her attention to detail and her ability to understand his needs, and he agreed to purchase the software system.

From that day forward, James became a loyal client, and he would often refer friends and colleagues to Sarika. She had won his trust and confidence through her active listening skills, and her business flourished as a result.

The Story of a Manager and Empathetic Listening

Sneha was a manager at a small marketing firm, and she was known for her ability to resolve conflicts between employees. One day, two of her team members, varun and Vasu came to her with a disagreement. They had been working on a project together, and they had different ideas on how to approach a certain task. The situation escalated quickly, and they were no longer speaking to each other.

Sneha listened carefully to each of them, and she could see that they were both passionate about their ideas. She asked questions, validated their feelings, and demonstrated empathy for their perspectives. Through her empathetic listening, Sneha was able to find common ground and resolve the conflict in a way that was fair to both Tom and Julie.

By the end of the meeting, varun and vasu were smiling and shaking hands, and they were eager to get back to work on the project. Sneha's empathetic listening had brought them together and improved their relationship.

The Story of a Customer Service Representative and Poor Listening Skills

1.Latha was a customer service representative for a large telecommunications company, and she was known for her poor listening skills. She was often impatient, interrupting her customers, and not paying attention to their concerns.

One day, Latha received a call from a customer named Ravi, who was having issues with his phone line.Ravi was frustrated and upset, and he was looking for a resolution to his problem. However, Latha's poor listening skills only made the situation worse. She interrupted Ravi repeatedly, and she didn't seem to be taking his concerns seriously.

Ravi ended the call feeling more frustrated than when he started, and he was not satisfied with the resolution to his problem. Latha's poor listening skills had negatively impacted her relationship with

Ravi, and he was unlikely to recommend the company to others in the future.

The story of Latha highlights the importance of being mindful of our listening habits and avoiding common mistakes such as interrupting or not paying attention. By improving our listening skills, we can build better relationships and improve the quality of our communication with others.

2. A young woman named Priya who works as a customer service representative in a call center. Priya was known for her polite and efficient handling of customer complaints. However, her supervisor noticed that she often cut customers off mid-sentence, which made them even more frustrated. When Priya's supervisor approached her about the issue, Priya was shocked. She had always thought she was a good listener and had no idea that her behavior was perceived as rude.

To help Priya improve her listening skills, her supervisor suggested she practice active listening. Priya learned that active listening meant paying full attention to the customer, making eye contact, and asking clarifying questions to fully understand their perspective. She also learned to slow down her thoughts and let the customer finish their sentences before responding.

With time and practice, Priya became an excellent active listener and was highly praised by her customers for her empathetic and understanding approach.

VIII

Effective Written Communication

In today's world, the ability to write with clarity, accuracy, and coherence is essential for success in almost any field.

When it comes to written communication, we often tend to focus on the choice of words. However, effective communication requires much more than just the selection of appropriate words. It involves the capacity to express ourselves clearly and precisely, while also considering the needs and expectations of our readers.

It is particularly critical to possess strong written communication skills in academic and professional contexts, where the stakes can be high. In such settings, writing that is poorly executed can lead to misunderstandings, missed opportunities, and even damaged reputations. On the other hand, writing that is clear, accurate, and engaging can open doors and create opportunities for success.

To be an effective communicator, it is important to consider the context and audience for your writing. For instance, the tone and formality that you might use in an email to a friend is quite different from that which would be appropriate for a report to your boss. Thus, having a deep understanding of your audience and the purpose of your writing can enable you to choose the appropriate style and level of formality.

Another vital aspect of writing effectively is organization. Your writing should have a clear structure, with a logical flow of ideas and supporting evidence. This will help your readers to understand your message and follow your argument.

Along with organization, effective communication requires attention to detail. This encompasses aspects such as spelling, grammar, and punctuation. Such details may appear minor, but they can have a significant impact on how your writing is received. Errors can distract your readers and undermine your credibility.

Finally, it is crucial to bear in mind that effective written communication is a skill that can be developed and improved with practice. As we move through this course, we will explore various strategies for enhancing your writing skills and applying them in academic and professional contexts.

Being able to write well is a fundamental skill that is essential for success in various domains. Understanding your audience and purpose, organizing your writing, paying attention to detail, and practicing your skills are all key ingredients for becoming a more effective communicator. I hope that this introduction has inspired you to reflect on the importance of effective writing and to start developing your own skills in this area.

When and When Not to Use WrittenCommunication

There are various situations where written communication may be the most appropriate method of conveying your message. For instance, written communication can be useful when you need to provide complex information or detailed instructions. In such cases, written communication can allow your audience to review the information at their own pace and refer back to it as needed.

Written communication can also be beneficial when you need to keep a record of the conversation. For instance, emails and memos can provide a written record of the communication, which can be useful in case of any disputes or misunderstandings.

Moreover, written communication can be helpful when the person or people you need to communicate with are not available at the same time as you. For instance, you can leave a message for someone to read at their convenience, which can save time and improve communication efficiency.

However, there are some circumstances where written communication may not be the most appropriate form of communication. For instance, when a situation requires immediate attention or when the matter is urgent, written communication may be too slow. In such cases, verbal communication may be more effective and efficient.

Similarly, when the topic is sensitive or emotional, written communication may not be the most appropriate form of communication. It can be difficult to convey tone and emotion in written communication, which can lead to misunderstandings or hurt feelings.

Additionally, there are times when face-to-face communication may be preferable over written communication. For example, when building relationships, face-to-face communication can help build rapport and trust. Similarly, when dealing with complex or nuanced information, face-to-face communication can enable immediate feedback and clarification.

Written communication can be an effective method of communication in various circumstances. It is essential to consider the context and audience of your communication, along with the nature of the information or message you wish to convey. There are times when written communication may be appropriate, and other times when alternative forms of communication, such as verbal or face-to-face communication, may be more effective. Ultimately, choosing the most appropriate method of communication can improve your effectiveness and achieve better outcomes.

Complexity of the Topic

Let us discuss the considerations that must be taken into account when deciding whether to use written communication for complex topics.

Written communication can be a useful tool for conveying complex information, but it is important to consider whether the topic is suitable for written communication. In some cases, a topic may be too complex to be adequately conveyed through written communication alone. For instance, some technical or scientific concepts may require visual aids, demonstrations, or verbal explanations to be properly understood.

Furthermore, the complexity of the topic may also have implications for the audience's level of understanding. It is important to consider the intended audience's level of familiarity with the topic and whether they have the necessary background knowledge to understand the written communication. If the intended audience lacks the required background knowledge, written communication may be insufficient and could result in misunderstandings.

On the other hand, there are some circumstances where written communication may be the most appropriate form of communication for complex topics. For example, written communication can provide a permanent record of the information, which can be referred back to and reviewed as needed. Additionally, written communication can enable the audience to review and reflect on the information at their own pace, which can be particularly helpful for complex topics.

However, it is important to consider the limitations of written communication when conveying complex information. Written communication can be limited in its ability to convey tone, context, and nuance, which can be particularly important for complex topics. Additionally, written communication can be prone to misinterpretation and misunderstandings, which can be exacerbated by the complexity of the topic.

The complexity of the topic should be carefully considered when deciding whether to use written communication. While written communication can be a useful tool for conveying complex information, it is important to consider the audience's level of understanding, the limitations of written communication, and whether the topic can be adequately conveyed through written communication alone. Ultimately, the most appropriate method of communication will depend on the particular circumstances and the desired outcome of the communication.

Here are some examples to illustrate how the complexity of a topic can affect the decision to use written communication:

Example 1: A complex scientific concept If you are trying to explain a complex scientific concept that involves technical language and precise definitions, it may be more appropriate to use written communication. Written communication can allow you to use charts, diagrams, and other visual aids to help convey complex ideas more clearly. Additionally, written communication can be useful when dealing with a technical audience that is familiar with the language and terminology used in the field.

Example 2: A sensitive interpersonal issue If you are dealing with a sensitive interpersonal issue, such as an employee performance problem or a conflict between coworkers, it may be more appropriate to use face-to-face communication. Written communication can be prone to misinterpretation and may not convey the emotional nuances of the situation. Additionally, face-to-face communication can allow for a more nuanced discussion of the issue and can help build trust and rapport with the other person.

Example 3: A legal contract If you are drafting a legal contract, it is almost always more appropriate to use written communication. Written communication allows for precise language and can ensure that all parties have a clear understanding of the terms of the contract. Additionally, written communication can be used to create a permanent record of the agreement, which can be useful in case of any disputes or misunderstandings in the future.

These examples illustrate how the complexity of a topic can affect the decision to use written communication. In some cases, written communication can be the best choice, particularly when dealing with technical or legal information. In other cases, face-to-face communication may be more appropriate, particularly when dealing with sensitive interpersonal issues or when emotional nuances need to be conveyed. The key is to carefully consider the context and audience and choose the most appropriate method of communication for the situation at hand.

Amount of Discussion' Required

Written communication can be an effective way to facilitate a discussion, but it is important to consider whether the amount of discussion required is suitable for written communication. In some cases, a topic may require a significant amount of back-and-forth discussion, which can be challenging to achieve through written communication alone.

Moreover, in certain discussions, face-to-face communication may be more appropriate. For instance, when building relationships, face-to-face communication can help build rapport and trust. Similarly, when dealing with complex or nuanced information, face-to-face communication can enable immediate feedback and clarification.

On the other hand, written communication can be an effective tool when the amount of discussion required is limited. For example, when providing feedback on a specific task or conveying a simple message, written communication can be efficient and effective. Similarly, when communicating with a large group, written communication can ensure that all members receive the same information in a consistent manner.

However, it is important to consider the limitations of written communication when facilitating a discussion. Written communication can be limited in its ability to convey tone, context, and nuance, which can be particularly important in discussions. Additionally, written communication can be prone to misinterpretation and misunderstandings, which can be exacerbated by the nature and amount of discussion required.

The amount of discussion required should be carefully considered when deciding whether to use written communication. While written communication can be a useful tool for facilitating discussion, it is important to consider the limitations of written communication, the nature of the discussion, and whether face-to-face communication may be more appropriate. Ultimately, the most appropriate method of communication will depend on the particular circumstances and the desired outcome of the communication.

Here are some examples to illustrate how the amount of discussion required can affect the decision to use written communication:

Example 1: A brief update If you need to provide a brief update on a project or task, it may be more appropriate to use written communication. Written communication allows for a quick and efficient transfer of information, without the need for a lengthy discussion. Additionally, written communication can be useful in situations where the recipient may need to refer back to the information at a later time.

Example 2: A complex decision If you need to make a complex decision that requires input from multiple parties, it may be more appropriate to use face-to-face communication. Face-to-face communication allows for a more nuanced discussion of the issue, and can help ensure that all parties have a clear understanding of the decision and its implications. Additionally, face-to-face communication can help build trust and rapport among the parties involved.

Example 3: A brainstorming session If you need to generate ideas for a new project or initiative, it may be more appropriate to use face-to-face communication. Brainstorming sessions often require a free flow of ideas and input from multiple parties, which can be difficult to achieve through written communication. Additionally, face-to-face communication can help generate energy and excitement around the project, which can be difficult to convey through written communication.

These examples illustrate how the amount of discussion required can affect the decision to use written communication. In some cases, written communication can be the best choice, particularly when a quick and efficient transfer of information is needed. In other cases, face-to-face communication may be more appropriate, particularly when complex decisions need to

shades of meaning.

Let us discuss the considerations that must be taken into account when deciding whether to use written communication for conveying shades of meaning.

Written communication can be a powerful tool for conveying shades of meaning, but it is important to consider whether the nuances of the message can be conveyed effectively through writing. In some cases, face-to-face communication or other forms of communication may be more appropriate for conveying subtle differences in meaning.

Furthermore, the limitations of written communication can also pose challenges for conveying shades of meaning. Written communication can be limited in its ability to convey tone and context, which can be crucial for accurately conveying shades of meaning. Additionally, the cultural background and context of the audience can also impact how a message is interpreted, making it even more difficult to convey shades of meaning through writing.

On the other hand, written communication can be an effective tool when conveying certain shades of meaning. For example, when dealing with formal or technical language, written communication can be more precise and unambiguous, allowing for more nuanced meanings to be conveyed. Similarly, when communicating with a large group, written communication can ensure that all members receive the same information with minimal distortion or misinterpretation.

However, it is important to consider the limitations of written communication when conveying shades of meaning. Written communication can be prone to misinterpretation and misunderstandings, which can be exacerbated by the nuances of the message. Additionally, written communication may not be appropriate when trying to convey emotions or sentiments, which are often better conveyed through face-to-face communication.

The shades of meaning should be carefully considered when deciding whether to use written communication. While written communication can be a powerful tool for conveying certain shades of meaning, it is important to consider the limitations of written communication, the context of the audience, and whether face-to-face communication may be more appropriate. Ultimately, the most appropriate method of communication will depend on the particular circumstances and the desired outcome of the communication.

Here are some examples to illustrate how shades of meaning can affect the decision to use written communication:

Example 1: A performance review If you are conducting a performance review for an employee, it may be more appropriate to use face-to-face communication. Written communication can be prone to misinterpretation, and may not convey the nuances of the situation, such as tone and body language. Additionally, face-to-face communication allows for a more nuanced discussion of the employee's performance and can help ensure that the employee has a clear understanding of any areas that need improvement.

Example 2: A marketing campaign If you are developing a marketing campaign, it may be more appropriate to use written communication. Written communication can allow for precise language and can ensure that the campaign messaging is consistent across all channels. Additionally, written communication can be useful in creating a permanent record of the campaign messaging, which can be useful for future reference.

Example 3: A negotiation If you are negotiating a complex business deal, it may be more appropriate to use face-to-face communication. Negotiations often involve subtle shades of meaning and nonverbal communication, which can be difficult to convey through written communication. Additionally, face-to-face communication allows for a more nuanced discussion of the terms of the deal, and can help build trust and rapport between the parties involved.

These examples illustrate how shades of meaning can affect the decision to use written communication. In some cases, face-to-face communication may be the best choice, particularly when dealing with interpersonal or negotiation situations that involve nuanced shades of meaning. In other cases, written communication may be more appropriate, particularly when dealing with precise language and the need for a permanent record of the information. The key is to carefully consider the context and audience, and choose the most appropriate method of communication for the situation at hand.

Formal communication

let us discuss the considerations that must be taken into account when deciding whether to use written communication for formal purposes.

Written communication can be a powerful tool for conveying formal messages, but it is important to consider whether the formality of the message is appropriate for written communication. In some cases, face-to-face communication may be more appropriate for conveying the formality and seriousness of the message, particularly when dealing with sensitive or delicate issues.

The choice of language and tone is crucial when conveying formality through written communication. The use of technical or specialized language can be effective in conveying a sense of expertise and formality, but it is important to ensure that the language is appropriate for the intended audience. Similarly, the use of a formal tone can help convey a sense of respect and professionalism, but it is important to strike a balance between formality and approachability.

On the other hand, written communication can be an effective tool for conveying formal messages in certain situations. For example, when dealing with legal documents, contracts, or other official documents, written communication is often the preferred method of communication due to its ability to be precise and unambiguous. Similarly, written communication can be used for conveying formal messages to large groups, ensuring that the message is consistent and reaches all members of the audience.

However, it is important to consider the limitations of written communication when conveying formal messages. Written communication can be prone to misinterpretation and misunderstandings, particularly when dealing with complex or technical information. Additionally, written communication may not be appropriate for conveying emotion or sentiment, which can be crucial in formal situations where building trust and establishing rapport is important.

Hence,written communication can be an effective tool for conveying formal messages, but it is important to carefully consider the context and audience when deciding whether to use written communication for formal purposes. The language and tone must be appropriate for the message and the audience, and it is important to strike a balance between formality and approachability. While written communication can be precise and unambiguous, it is important to consider the limitations of written communication, particularly when dealing with complex or technical information, or when conveying emotion or sentiment. Ultimately, the most appropriate method of communication will depend on the particular circumstances and the desired outcome of the communication.

Here are some examples to illustrate how formal communication can affect the decision to use written communication:

Example 1: A job offer If you are extending a job offer, it may be more appropriate to use written communication. Formal communication is often necessary in business situations, particularly when dealing with legal agreements such as employment contracts. Written communication allows for precise language and can ensure that all parties have a clear understanding of the terms of the offer.

Example 2: A legal agreement If you are creating a legal agreement, it is almost always necessary to use written communication. Legal agreements require precise language and are often subject to legal scrutiny, making written communication the best choice. Additionally, written communication allows for a permanent record of the agreement, which can be important in case of any future disputes.

Example 3: A board meeting If you are conducting a formal board meeting, it may be appropriate to use both written and face-to-face communication. Written communication can be used to distribute materials such as meeting agendas and minutes, while face-to-face communication can be used for more nuanced discussion of the issues at hand. Additionally, formal communication is often necessary in board meetings to ensure that all parties are on the same page and that decisions are properly documented.

These examples illustrate how formal communication can affect the decision to use written communication. In many cases, formal communication requires precise language and the need for a permanent record of the information. Written communication is often the best choice in such situations. However, in situations such as board meetings, a combination of written and face-to-face communication may be the most appropriate. The key is to carefully consider the context and audience, and choose the most appropriate method of communication for the situation at hand.

Writing Effectively

Introduction: Effective writing is the cornerstone of effective communication in the modern world. Whether you are writing for academic purposes, personal reasons, or professional situations, it is crucial to be able to express yourself in a clear and concise manner. Writing effectively involves understanding your audience, tailoring your writing style to suit the situation, and using language that is appropriate for the context. In this section, we will explore some key strategies for writing effectively, including the importance of clarity, organization, and concision.

Clarity: One of the most important aspects of effective writing is clarity. Writing that is unclear, confusing, or overly complex can make it difficult for your audience to understand your message. To write with clarity, it is important to use simple language, avoid jargon or technical terms that may be unfamiliar to your audience, and use concrete examples or analogies to help explain complex concepts. Additionally, it is important to be consistent in your use of language and to avoid using vague or ambiguous terms that can lead to confusion.

Organization: Another key aspect of effective writing is organization. Writing that is poorly organized can be difficult to follow, leading to a loss of interest or attention from your audience. To write with good organization, it is important to start with a clear outline or plan for your writing, and to ensure that each paragraph or section of your writing has a clear focus and purpose. Additionally, it is important to use transitions and signposts to guide your audience through your writing and to help them understand the relationship between different ideas.

Concision: In addition to clarity and organization, effective writing also involves concision. Writing that is overly verbose, redundant, or repetitive can be tedious for your audience to read and may detract from your message. To write with concision, it is important to be economical with your language, avoiding unnecessary words, phrases, or sentences. It is also important to edit and revise your writing carefully, looking for opportunities to streamline your message and make it more concise.

Effective writing is a critical skill for anyone who wishes to communicate effectively in today's world. Whether you are writing for academic, personal, or professional purposes, it is important to strive for clarity, organization, and concision in your writing. By understanding your audience, tailoring your writing style to suit the situation, and using language that is appropriate for the context, you can write effectively and ensure that your message is understood and appreciated by your intended audience.

Subject Lines

In today's fast-paced digital world, subject lines are one of the most important aspects of effective communication. Whether you are sending an email, a text message, or a social media post, your subject line is the first thing that your audience will see, and it can determine whether or not they will open or engage with your message. Writing effective subject lines involves understanding your audience, being clear and concise, and using language that is engaging and attention-grabbing.

Understanding Your Audience: One of the most important aspects of writing effective subject lines is understanding your audience. Who are you writing to? What are their interests, needs, and preferences? What is the context of your message? By understanding your audience, you can tailor your subject line to be more relevant and engaging to them. For example, if you are writing to a group of professionals, your subject line may need to be more formal and business-like. If you are writing to a group of friends, your subject line may be more casual and humorous.

Being Clear and Concise: Another key aspect of writing effective subject lines is being clear and concise. Your subject line should convey the most important information about your message in a few words or less. Avoid using vague or overly broad language that may not convey the intended message. Also, avoid using excessive punctuation, such as exclamation marks, which can come across as unprofessional or spammy.

Using Engaging Language: In addition to being clear and concise, effective subject lines should use engaging language that captures your audience's attention. This can include using questions, puns, or wordplay to pique their interest. You can also use power words, such as "free," "new," or "limited time," to create a sense of urgency or excitement. However, it is important to avoid using clickbait or deceptive language, which can lead to disappointment and loss of trust with your audience.

Put the Main Point First

Introduction: When writing any form of communication, it is important to get to the point quickly and efficiently. One effective way to do this is by putting the main point first. By doing so, you can capture your reader's attention and ensure that your message is clear and concise. This technique can be applied to various forms of writing, including emails, reports, and essays.

Benefits of Putting the Main Point First: There are several benefits to putting the main point first when writing. Firstly, it helps to grab the reader's attention and convey the most important information upfront. This is particularly important in situations where the reader may have limited time or attention span, such as in a business setting or when communicating with busy individuals. Secondly, putting the main point first can help to establish credibility and expertise by demonstrating that the writer is knowledgeable and confident about their message. Finally, it can also help to avoid confusion and misunderstanding by ensuring that the reader understands the main point of the communication from the outset.

Techniques for Putting the Main Point First: There are several techniques that can be used to effectively put the main point first when writing. These include using headlines, topic sentences, and summaries to introduce the main idea at the beginning of a communication. It is also important to use clear and concise language that conveys the main point effectively. Additionally, using bullet points or lists can help to break down complex information and make it more digestible for the reader.

Putting the main point first is a critical aspect of effective writing. By using techniques such as headlines, topic sentences, and summaries, writers can convey the main idea of their communication quickly and efficiently. This can help to grab the reader's attention, establish credibility, and avoid confusion. Whether writing for personal or professional purposes, taking the time to structure your communication in this way can make all the difference in the success of your message.

Know Your Audience

Introduction: When writing any form of communication, it is important to consider your audience. Understanding your audience and tailoring your writing to their needs and expectations is crucial for effective communication. This means taking into account their level of familiarity with the topic, their interests and concerns, and their expectations for the communication.

Importance of Knowing Your Audience: Knowing your audience is important for several reasons. Firstly, it helps to ensure that your message is relevant and meaningful to them. By understanding their interests and concerns, you can tailor your message to meet their needs and increase their engagement with the communication. Secondly, knowing your audience can help you to communicate more effectively by using language and tone that is appropriate for them. This means considering factors such as their level of education, age, and cultural background. Finally, knowing your audience can help you to anticipate their questions and concerns, and to address them proactively in your communication.

Techniques for Knowing Your Audience: There are several techniques that can be used to effectively know your audience when writing. These include researching your audience to learn more about their interests, concerns, and expectations. This can be done through online research, surveys, or interviews. Additionally, it is important to consider the context and purpose of the communication when tailoring it to the audience. For example, a business report may require a more formal tone and language than a personal email.

Knowing your audience is a critical aspect of effective writing. By tailoring your writing to their needs and expectations, you can increase the relevance and engagement of your message. Techniques such as researching your audience and considering the context and purpose of the communication can help you to achieve this. Whether writing for personal or professional purposes, taking the time to understand your audience can make all the difference in the success of your communication.

Organization of the Message

Introduction: When writing any form of communication, it is important to organize your message effectively. This means structuring your writing in a way that is clear, concise, and easy to follow. Effective organization can help to ensure that your message is received and understood by your audience.

Importance of Organizing Your Message: Organizing your message is important for several reasons. Firstly, it helps to ensure that your writing is clear and concise. This means structuring your writing in a logical and easy-to-follow manner, so that your audience can quickly understand your message. Secondly, effective organization can help to highlight the most important points of your message. By prioritizing your message and structuring it accordingly, you can ensure that your audience understands the key takeaways. Finally, organizing your message can help to make your writing more engaging and interesting. By breaking up your writing into sections, using headings and bullet points, you can create a more visually appealing and reader-friendly message.

Techniques for Organizing Your Message: There are several techniques that can be used to organize your message effectively. These include outlining your message before you start writing, using headings and subheadings to break up your writing, using bullet points to highlight important points, and using transition sentences to move between sections. Additionally, it is important to consider the purpose of your communication and tailor the organization of your message accordingly. For example, a persuasive argument may require a different organizational structure than a report.

Organizing your message is a critical aspect of effective writing. By structuring your writing in a clear and concise manner, you can ensure that your message is understood by your audience. Techniques such as outlining your message, using headings and subheadings, and using transition sentences can help you to achieve this. Whether writing for personal or professional purposes, taking the time to organize your message can make all the difference in the success of your communication.

IX

Group Discussion

"Brainstorming for success: The value of group discussions in driving productivity and efficient decision-making."

Group discussions are an essential tool for communication and decision-making. They allow for the exchange of ideas and perspectives from multiple individuals, leading to better solutions and more informed decisions.

For example, imagine a team at work is trying to come up with a new marketing campaign. If they were to only consider their own individual ideas, they may miss out on important perspectives and insights. However, if they have a group discussion, they can bounce ideas off each other and arrive at For example, imagine a team at work is trying to come up with a new marketing campaign. If they were to only consider their own individual ideas, they may miss out on important perspectives and insights. However, if they have a group discussion, they can bounce ideas off each other and arrive at a more comprehensive and effective campaign that takes into account different perspectives and approaches.

Group discussions also promote teamwork and collaboration. When individuals work together to discuss and solve a problem, they can build trust, establish common goals, and strengthen their working relationship. This can lead to increased productivity and more efficient decision-making in the future.

In addition, group discussions are a great way to develop communication and interpersonal skills. Participants have the opportunity to practice active listening, articulating their ideas effectively, and handling conflicts and diverse opinions in a respectful manner.

Group discussions serve various purposes in the context of job seeking and student life. For job seekers, they are often used by employers as a means of evaluating communication, collaboration, and problem-solving skills. In the academic setting, group discussions can enhance learning and promote the development of critical thinking and teamwork skills.

Types of Group Discussions:

One common way to categorize group discussions is based on their level of formality.

Formal Group Discussions are typically structured and organized, with set objectives and ground rules. They may be held in a corporate setting, such as a board meeting, where decisions are being made and business is being conducted. In these types of discussions, participants are expected to follow a specific agenda and adhere to certain protocols.

In contrast, Informal Group Discussions are more relaxed and spontaneous. These types of discussions may take place in a more casual setting, such as a brainstorming session or a coffee break chat with coworkers. The objective of informal group discussions is often to generate ideas, share opinions, and build relationships, rather than making formal decisions.

Another way to categorize group discussions is based on their purpose or focus.

For example, there are problem-solving discussions,

where the group is tasked with finding a solution to a particular issue.

There are also decision-making discussions, where the group is responsible for making a final determination on a particular matter.

There are also informational or educational discussions, where the group is focused on exchanging knowledge or learning new information.

A problem-solving group discussion

It is a collaborative process where a group of people come together to identify, analyze, and solve a specific problem. The objective of a problem-solving group discussion is to leverage the diverse perspectives, experiences, and skills of the group members to arrive at a creative and effective solution to the problem at hand.

The steps involved in a problem-solving group discussion typically include:

Identifying the problem: The first step is to clearly define the problem that needs to be solved. This involves gathering information, analyzing data, and identifying the root cause of the problem.

Brainstorming: Once the problem is defined, the group engages in a brainstorming session to generate a list of potential solutions. This is done through an open and collaborative discussion, where all group members are encouraged to share their ideas.

Evaluating alternatives: After the brainstorming session, the group evaluates each potential solution to determine its feasibility, benefits, and drawbacks. This is done through discussion, research, and analysis.

Selecting the best solution: Based on the evaluation, the group selects the best solution and develops a plan of action to implement it. This plan should include specific tasks, deadlines, and responsibilities for each group member.

Implementation: The final step is to implement the solution and monitor its progress. This may involve modifying the solution as needed to address any issues that arise during implementation.

A successful problem-solving group discussion requires active participation and engagement from all group members, clear and open communication, and a willingness to collaborate and compromise to arrive at the best solution.

A decision-making group discussion

It is a collaborative process where a group of people come together to make a specific decision. The objective of a decision-making group discussion is to leverage the diverse perspectives, experiences, and skills of the group members to arrive at a well-informed and effective decision.

The steps involved in a decision-making group discussion typically include:

Defining the decision: The first step is to clearly define the decision that needs to be made. This involves gathering information, analyzing data, and identifying the goals and objectives of the decision.

Brainstorming: Once the decision is defined, the group engages in a brainstorming session to generate a list of potential options. This is done through an open and collaborative discussion, where all group members are encouraged to share their ideas.

Evaluating alternatives: After the brainstorming session, the group evaluates each potential option to determine its feasibility, benefits, and drawbacks. This is done through discussion, research, and analysis.

Selecting the best option: Based on the evaluation, the group selects the best option and develops a plan of action to implement it. This plan should include specific tasks, deadlines, and responsibilities for each group member.

Making the decision: The final step is to make the decision and implement the plan of action. The group should also establish a process for monitoring the decision and assessing its impact over time.

A successful decision-making group discussion requires active participation and engagement from all group members, clear and open communication, and a willingness to collaborate and compromise to arrive at the best decision. It is also important for the group to consider ethical, legal, and moral considerations in the decision-making process.

Informational or educational discussions are group discussions that are designed to impart knowledge and understanding about a particular topic. The main objective of these discussions is to provide participants with information that will help them make informed decisions, solve problems, or simply learn about a topic of interest.

The steps involved in an informational or educational group discussion typically include:

Defining the topic: The first step is to clearly define the topic that will be discussed. This involves identifying the key goals and objectives of the discussion, as well as the specific information that will be covered.

Preparing the information: The facilitator or leader of the discussion should gather and prepare the necessary information and materials to be presented during the discussion. This may include slides, handouts, or other resources.

Presenting the information: The facilitator or leader then presents the information to the group, using visual aids, examples, and other techniques to help the participants understand the topic.

Engaging the group: After the information has been presented, the facilitator or leader should engage the group in a discussion to allow participants to ask questions, clarify misunderstandings, and provide feedback.

Reinforcing the learning: The final step is to reinforce the learning that took place during the discussion. This may involve summarizing key points, providing additional resources, or conducting follow-up activities to help participants internalize the information.

A successful informational or educational group discussion requires clear and effective presentation of information, active engagement and participation from all group members, and a supportive and inclusive learning environment. It is also important for the facilitator or leader to adapt the discussion to the needs and interests of the group, and to maintain a focus on the goals and objectives of the discussion.

Team building discussions

Team building discussions are a type of group discussion that are focused on improving team cohesion, communication, and collaboration. These discussions are often used in workplace settings, and can be an effective way to help teams work more effectively together. Here are some tips to keep in mind when conducting team building discussions:

Set clear goals: Before the discussion, make sure that you have a clear understanding of what you hope to achieve. This could involve improving team morale, addressing specific team challenges, or improving communication and collaboration.

Encourage active participation: Encourage all team members to actively participate in the discussion. This can help to build trust and foster a sense of teamwork.

Foster open communication: Encourage open and honest communication during the discussion. This can help team members to share their thoughts and ideas, and to better understand the perspectives of their colleagues.

Encourage creativity: Encourage team members to think outside the box and to offer creative solutions to the challenges that the team is facing.

Celebrate successes: Take the time to celebrate the successes and achievements of the team during the discussion. This can help to build morale and foster a sense of team spirit.

By using these strategies, you can conduct effective team building discussions that help to improve team cohesion, communication, and collaboration.

Group Discussion vs. Individual Discussion

Group Discussions and Individual Discussions are two different methods of communication, each with its own strengths and weaknesses.

Group Discussions allow for the exchange of multiple perspectives and ideas, leading to better decision-making and problem-solving. They promote teamwork and collaboration, as well as the development of communication and interpersonal skills. When a group discusses a problem or decision, each person has the opportunity to share their thoughts and insights, which can lead to a more well-rounded and informed solution.

However, Group Discussions can also be time-consuming and may require more effort to coordinate and organize. There may also be the potential for disagreements or conflicts to arise, which can slow down the discussion process.

Individual Discussions, on the other hand, are limited to one person's perspective and ideas. They can be quicker and more efficient in decision-making, as the individual has complete control over the conversation and can make a determination without the need for consensus.

However, Individual Discussions lack the diversity of perspectives and ideas that can be achieved through a group discussion. The individual may also miss out on important insights or considerations that could have been brought up in a group setting.

Preparation for Group Discussions

Importance of research and preparation

Preparing for group discussions is crucial to ensuring that you are able to effectively participate and contribute to the discussion. Research and preparation can help you to understand the context of the discussion, familiarize yourself with the topic, and be prepared to contribute to the discussion in a meaningful way.

Here are some steps that you can take to prepare for a group discussion:

Research the topic: Before the discussion, research the topic thoroughly. This could involve reading relevant articles, watching videos, or speaking with experts in the field.

Familiarize yourself with the company or organization: If you are participating in a group discussion as part of a job interview, research the company or organization beforehand. This will help you to understand their mission, values, and goals, and to better understand the context of the discussion.

Practice your communication skills: Effective communication is a key component of successful group discussions. Practice speaking clearly, actively listening to others, and expressing your ideas and opinions in a clear and concise manner.

Collaborate with others: If possible, practice collaborating with others before the discussion. This will help you to become more comfortable working as part of a team and to build your skills in contributing to group discussions.

By taking these steps, you will be well-prepared for your group discussion and will be able to participate effectively, making a positive contribution to the discussion.

Suggestions for researching the company or topic in advance

Researching the company or topic in advance is a crucial step in preparing for a group discussion. Here are some suggestions for conducting effective research:

Review the company website: The company's website is a great starting point for learning about the organization. Look for information about their mission, values, and goals, as well as information about the products and services they offer.

Look for industry news: Stay informed about the latest news and developments in the industry by reading relevant articles and reports.

Speak with experts: If possible, reach out to experts in the field and ask for their perspectives on the topic or company.

Utilize social media: Follow the company or relevant industry organizations on social media to stay informed about the latest news and developments.

Participate in online forums: Join online forums and discussion groups related to the topic or industry to gain insights from others.

By conducting thorough research, you will be well-prepared to participate in the group discussion and contribute effectively. It will also demonstrate your interest and commitment to the topic or company, which can be a positive factor in the discussion.

Tips for practicing effective communication and collaboration skills

Effective communication and collaboration skills are critical for success in group discussions. Here are some tips for practicing these skills:

Practice active listening: Pay attention to what others are saying and show that you are engaged in the conversation by nodding, asking questions, and summarizing their points.

Enhance your nonverbal communication skills: Nonverbal cues such as eye contact, body language, and facial expressions can greatly impact the effectiveness of your communication.

Develop strong presentation skills: The ability to articulate your thoughts and ideas clearly and concisely is important in group discussions. Practice speaking in front of others and receive feedback to improve your presentation skills.

Collaborate with others: Participate in group projects, team building activities, and volunteer opportunities to build your collaboration skills.

Seek feedback: Ask for feedback from others on your communication and collaboration skills. This can help you identify areas for improvement and enhance your abilities in these areas.

By consistently practicing these skills, you can become a more effective communicator and collaborator, which will serve you well in group discussions and other professional and personal settings.

Strategies for Success in Group Discussions

Setting Objectives and Ground Rules for Group Discussions

When setting objectives, it's important to be clear and specific about what the group hopes to achieve through the discussion. This could include making a decision, generating ideas, exchanging information, or improving understanding of a particular issue. Having a clear objective will help focus the discussion and ensure that everyone is on the same page.

Ground Rules, on the other hand, establish the expectations for behavior and participation during the discussion. This could include guidelines such as allowing everyone to speak, avoiding interruptions, keeping the discussion on topic, or maintaining a respectful tone. Having ground rules in place can help to ensure that the discussion remains productive and respectful, and that everyone has an equal opportunity to participate.

It's important to establish both objectives and ground rules at the beginning of the discussion, and to revisit them as needed to ensure that everyone is still aligned and the discussion is on track. It's also important to make sure that all participants understand and agree to the objectives and ground rules, as this will help to ensure a successful and productive discussion.

Understanding Group Dynamics

A successful group discussion requires an understanding of the dynamics of group communication. This means being aware of the various factors that influence how a group interacts and communicates, and how these factors can impact the success of the discussion. Some of the key dynamics to consider include:

Group size: The size of the group can have a significant impact on the dynamics of the discussion. For example, larger groups may lead to more diverse perspectives and ideas, but they may also make it more difficult to reach a consensus.

Group composition: The backgrounds and personalities of the group members can also play a role in the dynamics of the discussion. For example, diverse perspectives can lead to more creative solutions, while conflicting personalities can create tension and difficulties in reaching consensus.

Leadership: The leadership style of the facilitator or group leader can also impact the dynamics of the discussion. For example, an authoritative leader may be effective in maintaining control and focus, but may also stifle creativity and participation.

Group norms and culture: The group's norms and culture can influence how members interact and communicate. For example, a group with a strong culture of respect and collaboration may be more effective in promoting positive and constructive discussions.

By being aware of these dynamics and how they can impact the discussion, you can better prepare for and participate in group discussions in a way that contributes to their success.

Best practices for actively listening and contributing to the discussion

Active listening and contributing are crucial skills for success in group discussions. Here are some best practices to keep in mind:

Pay attention: Focus on what is being said and try to understand the perspectives and opinions of others. Avoid distractions and be present in the moment.

Ask questions: Encourage others to share their thoughts by asking open-ended questions and clarifying what they mean.

Avoid interrupting: Allow others to fully express their ideas and opinions before responding. Interrupting can be seen as disrespectful and can create tension in the discussion.

Listen with empathy: Try to understand the feelings and emotions behind what is being said. This can help to build rapport and create a more positive and productive discussion.

Offer insights and opinions: Share your own thoughts and ideas, but do so in a way that is respectful and constructive. Avoid being aggressive or dismissive of others' opinions.

Summarize and restate: Periodically summarize what has been said to ensure that everyone is on the same page and to facilitate a clearer and more productive discussion.

By actively listening and contributing in a thoughtful and respectful manner, you can help to create a positive and productive group discussion.

Techniques for effectively expressing ideas and opinions

Expressing your ideas and opinions effectively is a key component of success in group discussions. Here are some techniques that can help:

Be clear and concise: Clearly articulate your ideas and opinions in a way that is easy to understand. Avoid using jargon or overly complex language.

Support your ideas with evidence: Use data, statistics, examples, or other forms of evidence to support your arguments. This makes your ideas more convincing and helps others to see your point of view.

Use effective body language: Your nonverbal cues, such as eye contact, facial expressions, and gestures, can have a big impact on how your ideas are received. Use confident and assertive body language to convey your ideas effectively.

Speak with conviction: Speak with confidence and conviction, but avoid being overly aggressive or confrontational. A calm and measured tone can help to build trust and credibility.

Practice active listening: Make sure to actively listen to others and incorporate their ideas into your own thoughts and opinions. This helps to create a collaborative and inclusive discussion.

By using these techniques, you can effectively express your ideas and opinions in a group discussion and contribute to a positive and productive outcome.

Handling conflicts and difficult personalities

Conflicts and difficult personalities can sometimes arise in group discussions, and it's important to have strategies in place for handling these challenges. Here are some tips to keep in mind:

Remain calm: When dealing with conflict or difficult personalities, it's important to remain calm and composed. This will help to de-escalate the situation and prevent it from becoming more heated.

Identify the root cause: Try to understand the underlying issue or concern that is causing the conflict or difficulty. This can help you to address the problem more effectively.

Use active listening: Listen actively to what the other person is saying, and try to understand their perspective. This can help to build rapport and resolve the conflict.

Be respectful: Speak and act in a respectful manner, even when dealing with a difficult personality. Avoid using aggressive or confrontational language, and instead opt for a calm and measured approach.

Seek common ground: Look for areas of common ground or shared goals, and try to find ways to work together towards a solution.

Seek outside help: If the situation becomes particularly challenging, don't be afraid to seek outside help. This could involve bringing in a mediator, seeking the advice of a mentor, or finding other resources to support the discussion.

By using these strategies, you can effectively handle conflicts and difficult personalities in group discussions, and help to create a positive and productive outcome.

Articulating Ideas Clearly and Effectively

Articulating ideas clearly and effectively is an important Communication Skill in Group Discussions. When you are able to articulate your ideas clearly, it helps to ensure that everyone in the group understands what you are trying to convey. This, in turn, can lead to more productive and respectful discussions.

To articulate ideas clearly and effectively in group discussions, try the following tips:

Know your message: Be clear about what you want to say before you begin speaking.

Use simple language: Avoid using technical terms or jargon that others may not understand.

Be concise: Speak in short, clear sentences that are easy to understand.

Use examples: Provide concrete examples to help illustrate your ideas.

Speak with confidence: Speak clearly and confidently, and avoid filler words such as "um" and "ah".

Engage the group: Ask for feedback and engage the group in a dialogue about your ideas.

Use visual aids: Use visual aids, such as slides or handouts, to help illustrate your ideas.

By articulating your ideas clearly and effectively in group discussions, you can help to ensure that your message is understood and that the discussion remains productive and respectful. Additionally, when everyone in the group is able to articulate their ideas clearly, it helps to build a collaborative and supportive environment that encourages discussion and new ideas.

Encouraging and Responding to Different Views

Encouraging and Responding to Different Views is an important Communication Skill in Group Discussions. It helps to promote diversity of thought and encourages everyone to participate in the discussion, even if they have different perspectives. This can lead to more creative and innovative solutions, and help to build a more inclusive and respectful group dynamic.

To encourage and respond to different views in group discussions, try the following tips:

Create a safe space: Encourage everyone to participate, and create an environment where everyone feels comfortable sharing their opinions.

Listen actively: Pay attention to what others are saying, and avoid interrupting or speaking over others.

Show respect: Acknowledge others' perspectives, even if you disagree with them.

Ask questions: Ask questions to encourage others to share more information and to deepen the discussion.

Avoid personal attacks: Focus on the issue, not the person. Avoid making personal attacks or belittling others' opinions.

Seek common ground: Look for areas of agreement and build on them.

Respecting Diversity and Avoiding Conflicts

Respecting Diversity and Avoiding Conflicts are critical components of effective Communication Skills in Group Discussions. When everyone in the group is respectful and avoids conflicts, it helps to create a supportive and inclusive environment that encourages discussion and collaboration.

To respect diversity and avoid conflicts in group discussions, try the following tips:

Be inclusive: Encourage everyone to participate, and create an environment where everyone feels comfortable sharing their opinions.

Show respect: Acknowledge others' perspectives, even if you disagree with them.

Avoid personal attacks: Focus on the issue, not the person. Avoid making personal attacks or belittling others' opinions.

Seek common ground: Look for areas of agreement and build on them.

Embrace diversity: Embrace diversity of thought and encourage everyone to participate, even if they have different perspectives.

Address conflicts constructively: If conflicts do arise, address them in a constructive manner. Listen to each other, seek to understand the other person's perspective, and find a solution that works for everyone.

Focus on the issue: When discussing controversial issues, focus on the issue, not the person. Avoid making personal attacks or belittling others' opinions.

Keeping the Discussion On-topic and Focused

Keeping the Discussion On-topic and Focused is a critical component of effective Communication Skills in Group

Discussions. When discussions are on-topic and focused, everyone in the group can contribute to the conversation, and the group can achieve its goals more effectively.

To keep the discussion on-topic and focused in group discussions, try the following tips:

Set clear objectives: Before the discussion begins, set clear objectives for what the group hopes to achieve.

Stay on topic: Encourage everyone to stay on topic and avoid allowing the discussion to wander or get sidetracked.

Encourage participation: Encourage everyone to participate and avoid letting one person dominate the discussion.

Ask open-ended questions: Ask open-ended questions that encourage discussion and exploration of different perspectives.

Summarize key points: Regularly summarize the key points that have been discussed to ensure that everyone is on the same page and the discussion remains focused.

End on a positive note: End the discussion on a positive note, by summarizing what the group has achieved and what steps will be taken next.

Do's and Don'ts of Group Discussions:

Here are some general do's and don'ts to keep in mind when participating in a group discussion:

Do's:

Prepare in advance: Research the topic and familiarize yourself with the discussion's objectives, as well as the backgrounds and perspectives of other participants.

Listen actively: Pay attention to what others are saying, ask clarifying questions, and acknowledge their perspectives and contributions.

Speak clearly and concisely: Make sure your ideas are well-articulated and easy for others to understand.

Be open-minded: Be willing to consider other people's opinions and viewpoints, even if they differ from your own.

Respect others: Treat others with respect and avoid interrupting or talking over them.

Be a team player: Collaborate with others and work together to find solutions or reach a consensus.

Don'ts:

Dominate the conversation: Don't monopolize the discussion or speak for extended periods without allowing others to participate.

Be aggressive or confrontational: Avoid arguing or being confrontational with others. Instead, use constructive language to express your views and resolve conflicts.

Interrupt others: Respect others' turns to speak and avoid interrupting them.

Be negative or dismissive: Avoid being negative or dismissive of others' ideas and contributions. Instead, encourage positive and constructive discussions.

Show disinterest: Avoid appearing disinterested or disengaged during the discussion. Instead, be present and actively participate.

By following these do's and don'ts, you can help create a productive and respectful group discussion environment where everyone's contributions are valued and encouraged.

X

Interview skills

"Making a lasting impression: Showcasing confidence, competence, and communication skills in a job interview."

Introduction

Interviews play a crucial role in the hiring process for many organizations. They provide employers with the opportunity to assess a candidate's qualifications, skills, and personality, and determine if they are a good fit for the job and the company. It is therefore essential for job seekers to understand the purpose of an interview and to be prepared for the interview process. In this chapter, we will discuss the purpose of an interview, the importance of preparation, and the benefits of mastering interview skills.

The purpose of an interview is to determine if a candidate is the right fit for a job and the company. During an interview, employers evaluate a candidate's qualifications, work experience, and skills, as well as their personality and how well they communicate. The interview is also an opportunity for the candidate to learn more about the job and the company, and to ask questions about the role and the organization.

"Do Your Homework: Preparation is key to success in an interview. Understanding the employer's perspective and researching the company can give you a competitive edge and help you stand out as a strong candidate."

The Importance of Preparation for an Interview

Preparation is key to a successful interview. A well-prepared candidate is more likely to perform well in the interview and make a positive impression on the employer. This includes researching the company and the job, preparing responses to common interview questions, dressing appropriately, and practicing good communication and interpersonal skills. By preparing for an interview, you can reduce stress and anxiety, increase your confidence, and increase your chances of getting the job.

The Benefits of Mastering Interview Skills

Mastering interview skills can have a positive impact on your career. It can help you make a positive impression on potential employers, increase your chances of getting hired, and lead to better job opportunities in the future. By understanding the purpose of an interview, preparing for the interview process, and developing strong interview skills, you can improve your chances of success and achieve your career goals.

"Fear and anxiety overshadowing their confidence before the big interview."

Overcoming fear and anxiety in job interviews: The interview process can be nerve-wracking, causing fear and anxiety to overshadow even the most confident of individuals. However, it's important to remember that preparation, self-reflection, and a positive attitude can help overcome these feelings and allow you to showcase your skills and qualities to potential employers.

The Purpose of an Interview

Understanding the Employer's Perspective

Understanding the employer's perspective is crucial to preparing for and performing well in an interview. When preparing for an interview, it is important to understand what the employer is looking for in a candidate, and to tailor your responses accordingly. Some common factors that employers consider during the interview process include:

Relevant work experience and qualifications: Employers want to know that a candidate has the skills and experience necessary to perform the job successfully. They may ask about your past work experiences, projects you have worked on, and your education and qualifications.

Communication and interpersonal skills: Employers want to see that a candidate can communicate effectively, both verbally and in writing. They also want to see that a candidate can work well with others, build positive relationships with coworkers, and collaborate effectively on projects.

Problem-solving skills: Employers want to see that a candidate can identify and solve problems in a creative and effective manner. They may ask about specific examples of how you have tackled problems in the past and how you handle challenges.

Positive attitude and motivation: Employers want to see that a candidate is enthusiastic about the job, has a positive attitude, and is motivated to succeed. They may ask about your

What Employers Look for in a Candidate

When evaluating candidates during an interview, employers look for a combination of technical skills, experience, and personal qualities. Some of the most important qualities that employers look for in a candidate include:

Relevant work experience and qualifications: Employers want to see that a candidate has the necessary experience and education to perform the job successfully. They may ask about your past work experiences, projects you have worked on, and your education and qualifications.

Communication and interpersonal skills: Good communication skills are essential in most jobs, and employers want to see that a candidate can communicate effectively both verbally and in writing. They also want to see that a candidate can work well with others, build positive relationships with coworkers, and collaborate effectively on projects.

Problem-solving skills: Employers want to see that a candidate can identify and solve problems in a creative and effective manner. They may ask about specific examples of how you have tackled problems in the past and how you handle challenges.

Positive attitude and motivation: Employers want to see that a candidate is enthusiastic about the job, has a positive attitude, and is motivated to succeed. They may ask about your goals, why you are interested in the job, and what you hope to achieve in the role.

Adaptability and flexibility: Employers want to see that a candidate can adjust to change and work effectively in different situations. They may ask about how you have handled change or ambiguity in the past, and how you handle stress and challenges.

Team player qualities: Employers want to see that a candidate can work effectively as part of a team, and contribute to a positive and productive work environment. They may ask about your experience working with teams, and how you handle conflict or disagreements with coworkers.

Good organizational and time management skills: Employers want to see that a candidate can manage their time effectively, prioritize tasks, and meet deadlines. They may ask about your approach to organization and time management, and give you scenarios to see how you would prioritize tasks.

Understanding the Job Requirements

Understanding the job requirements is an important step in preparing for an interview. This will help you determine if the job is a good fit for you, and it will also help you prepare for the interview by highlighting your relevant skills and experience. Here are some steps to help you understand the job requirements:

Read the job description and requirements carefully: Review the job description and requirements in detail to get a clear understanding of what the employer is looking for in a candidate. Take note of the specific skills and experience required for the job, as well as any other requirements such as certifications, language proficiency, and education.

Research the company: Research the company to get a better understanding of its culture, values, and goals. This will help you tailor your responses during the interview to align with the company's priorities and values.

Ask questions: If there is anything you are unclear about in the job description or requirements, don't hesitate to ask the employer for clarification. This will demonstrate your interest in the job and your commitment to understanding what is expected of you.

By understanding the job requirements and researching the company, you will be better equipped to prepare for the interview and highlight how your skills and experience match what the employer is looking for.

Do's of an Interview

Researching the company

Researching the company is one of the most important do's of an interview. Doing so will not only help you better understand the company's culture, values, and goals, but it will also demonstrate your interest in the job and your commitment to the interview process. Here are some steps to help you research the company:

Visit the company website: Start by visiting the company's website to get an overview of its products, services, and mission. Take note of any recent news or events related to the company, as well as any information about its leadership and history.

Check social media: Follow the company on social media platforms such as LinkedIn, Twitter, and Facebook to get a sense of its company culture and to see any updates or news.

Read recent press releases: Look for recent press releases and articles about the company to get a better understanding of its current initiatives and plans for the future.

Ask for information: If you know someone who works at the company, consider reaching out to them to ask for their perspective on the company culture, values, and goals. You can also ask the interviewer for more information about the company during the interview.

By researching the company, you will be better equipped to answer questions about why you are interested in the job, and you will also be able to tailor your responses to align with the company's priorities and values.

Dressing Appropriately

Dressing appropriately is another important do of an interview. Your attire should be professional, clean, and appropriate for the type of job you are interviewing for. Here are some tips to help you dress appropriately for an interview:

Know the dress code: Research the company's dress code and aim to dress one step above the expected level of attire. For example, if the dress code is business casual, consider dressing in business attire.

Choose professional attire: Wear clothes that are clean, pressed, and in good condition. Avoid wearing clothes that are too tight, too revealing, or too casual.

Avoid overly flashy or distracting accessories: Stick to neutral colors and understated accessories, such as a watch and a simple necklace or earrings. Avoid wearing anything that could be seen as distracting or too flashy.

Make sure your shoes are polished: Your shoes should be clean and polished, and they should match your attire.

Be well-groomed: Make sure your hair is neat and clean, and that you are clean-shaven or have neatly trimmed facial hair. Wear minimal make-up and avoid wearing overpowering fragrances.

By dressing appropriately, you will show the employer that you are taking the interview seriously and that you respect their company culture and values.

Arriving On Time

Arriving on time is a critical do of an interview. Being punctual demonstrates your professionalism, respect for the employer's time, and your overall reliability. Here are some tips to help you arrive on time for an interview:

Plan ahead: Research the location of the interview, and plan your route accordingly. Allow extra time for unexpected traffic, parking, or other delays.

Set an alarm: Set an alarm or reminders on your phone to ensure you don't oversleep or get caught up in other tasks and forget about the interview.

Leave early: Give yourself enough time to arrive at the interview location early, allowing for unexpected delays or issues. Arriving 15 minutes early is a good rule of thumb.

Notify the employer of any delays: If you are running late or anticipate being late, call or email the employer as soon as possible to let them know. Offer an explanation for the delay and apologize for any inconvenience.

By arriving on time, you will show the employer that you are responsible, reliable, and respectful of their time. This can make a positive impression and increase your chances of being offered the job.

Positive Body Language

Positive body language is another important do of an interview. Your body language can communicate a lot about your confidence, interest, and engagement, and can have a significant impact on the impression you make. Here are some tips for demonstrating positive body language during an interview:

Maintain eye contact: Maintaining eye contact with the interviewer shows that you are engaged, confident, and interested in what they are saying. Avoid looking down, away, or at your phone during the interview.

Smile: A smile can convey warmth, friendliness, and approachability. Smile when you greet the interviewer and when you are answering questions.

Sit up straight: Good posture conveys confidence and a professional demeanor. Sit up straight, with your shoulders back and your feet flat on the floor.

Use gestures: Appropriate gestures can help convey your ideas and emotions. Avoid fidgeting or making nervous gestures, such as playing with your hair or tapping your foot.

Listen actively: Demonstrate your interest and engagement by nodding, making appropriate facial expressions, and using appropriate verbal cues, such as "uh-huh" or "I see."

By demonstrating positive body language, you will show the employer that you are confident, interested, and engaged in the interview process. This can help increase your chances of making a positive impression and ultimately landing the job.

Active Listening

Active listening is an important do of an interview. It involves paying close attention to the interviewer's questions and responses, and demonstrating your understanding and engagement through verbal and nonverbal cues. Here are some tips for actively listening during an interview:

Focus your attention: Eliminate distractions, such as your phone or other electronic devices, and give the interviewer your full attention.

Ask clarifying questions: If you don't understand a question or need more information, don't be afraid to ask for clarification. This demonstrates your engagement and interest in the process.

Repeat key points: Paraphrasing the interviewer's questions and key points can demonstrate your understanding and help you stay focused.

Take notes: Taking notes during the interview can help you remember important details and keep you focused. Just be sure to ask the interviewer if it's okay before you start taking notes.

Show your interest: Use verbal and nonverbal cues, such as nodding or making appropriate facial expressions, to show your interest and engagement in the conversation.

By actively listening, you will show the employer that you are interested, engaged, and taking the interview seriously. This can increase your chances of making a positive impression and ultimately landing the job.

Asking Informed Questions

Asking informed questions during an interview is another important do. It shows the employer that you have done your research, are interested in the company and the role, and are engaged in the interview process. Here are some tips for asking informed questions during an interview:

Research the company: Before the interview, research the company and the role you are applying for. This will help you ask informed questions and demonstrate your interest in the company.

Prepare a list of questions: Make a list of questions to ask during the interview. This can help you stay organized and focused, and ensure that you don't forget to ask important questions.

Ask about the company culture: Ask questions about the company culture, such as what the company values or what a typical day is like for employees.

Ask about the role: Ask questions about the role, such as what the responsibilities are, what the potential for growth is, or what kind of support the company offers.

Ask about next steps: At the end of the interview, ask the interviewer about next steps, such as when you can expect to hear back about the decision or what the timeline is for the hiring process.

By asking informed questions, you will show the employer that you have done your research, are interested in the company and the role, and are engaged in the interview process. This can increase your chances of making a positive impression and ultimately landing the job

Following Up After the Interview

Following up after the interview is another important do. It shows the employer that you are professional, interested in the role, and respectful of their time. Here are some tips for following up after an interview:

Send a thank-you note: Send a thank-you note or email to the interviewer within 24 to 48 hours of the interview. This is a great opportunity to reiterate your interest in the role and thank the interviewer for their time.

Be prompt: Follow up in a timely manner, within the timeline that the interviewer specified or within a reasonable time frame if they did not specify.

Reiterate your interest: Reiterate your interest in the role and the company, and express your enthusiasm for the opportunity.

Address any concerns: If the interviewer raised any concerns during the interview, address them in your follow-up. This can demonstrate your problem-solving skills and your commitment to finding a solution.

Be professional: Follow-up in a professional and respectful manner, and avoid being too pushy or aggressive.

By following up after the interview, you will show the employer that you are professional, interested in the role, and respectful of their time. This can increase your chances of making a positive impression and ultimately landing the job.

Don'ts of an Interview

Being Late

Being late to an interview is a major don't. It shows the employer that you are not reliable, and it can create a negative impression before the interview even starts. Here are some tips for avoiding being late to an interview:

Plan ahead: Allow yourself plenty of time to get to the interview, factoring in traffic, parking, and other potential delays.

Check the location: Before the interview, check the location and make sure you know how to get there. If possible, do a dry run of the route ahead of time.

Set an alarm: Set an alarm or reminders to ensure you don't oversleep or forget about the interview.

Be proactive: If you know you are running late, call the interviewer and let them know. Apologize for the delay and explain the situation, and ask if it's still possible to reschedule.

By avoiding being late, you will show the employer that you are reliable and professional, and increase your chances of making a positive impression.

Dressing Inappropriately

Dressing inappropriately for an interview is another major don't. It shows the employer that you are not taking the interview seriously, and it can create a negative impression. Here are some tips for dressing appropriately for an interview:

Research the company: Before the interview, research the company and the role you are applying for. This will give you an idea of the dress code and help you dress appropriately.

Dress conservatively: For most interviews, it's best to dress conservatively and professionally. This usually means wearing a suit or dress pants and a dress shirt or blouse.

Pay attention to details: Make sure your clothing is clean, pressed, and free of holes or tears. Wear polished shoes and avoid wearing too much jewelry or makeup.

Consider the role: If you are applying for a role in a creative industry, such as fashion or design, you may be able to dress more creatively. However, it's still important to dress professionally and avoid anything too bold or distracting.

By dressing appropriately for an interview, you will show the employer that you are taking the interview seriously, and increase your chances of making a positive impression.

Being Negative or Critical of Past Employers

Being negative or critical of past employers is another major don't in an interview. It shows the employer that you may be difficult to work with, and it can create a negative impression. Here are some tips for avoiding being negative or critical of past employers:

Focus on the positives: When talking about past employers, focus on the positive aspects of your experience, such as the skills you developed or the projects you worked on.

Avoid negativity: Avoid speaking negatively about past employers or colleagues, even if you had a difficult experience. Instead, try to be neutral and professional.

Show growth: If you were let go from a past role, use the opportunity to talk about what you learned from the experience and how you have grown since then.

Stay focused: Stay focused on the present and the future, and avoid dwelling on the past. Show the interviewer that you are looking forward to new opportunities and that you are excited about the role you are applying for.

By avoiding negativity and criticism of past employers, you will show the employer that you are professional and respectful, and increase your chances of making a positive impression.

Talking Too Much or Too Little

Talking too much or too little during an interview is another common pitfall. It can be difficult to strike the right balance, but it's important to avoid talking too much or too little, as it can create a negative impression. Here are some tips for avoiding this common mistake:

Prepare: Before the interview, think about the key points you want to make, and practice answering common interview questions. This will help you feel more confident and avoid talking too much or too little.

Listen: During the interview, listen to the interviewer's questions and try to answer them directly and concisely. Avoid rambling or going off on tangents.

Ask questions: If you are worried about talking too little, ask informed questions about the company or the role. This will show the interviewer that you are engaged and interested, and help keep the conversation flowing.

Take your time: If you are worried about talking too much, take a deep breath and take your time before answering questions. This will help you stay calm and focused, and avoid talking too much.

By avoiding talking too much or too little, you will show the interviewer that you are confident and professional, and increase your chances of making a positive impression.

Not Having a Clear Understanding of the Job Requirements

Not having a clear understanding of the job requirements is another common mistake in an interview. This can make it difficult to answer questions about why you are interested in the role and what you can bring to the company. Here are some tips for avoiding this mistake:

Research the company: Before the interview, research the company and the role you are applying for. This will give you a better understanding of the job requirements and help you prepare.

Read the job description: Make sure you have read the job description carefully and have a clear understanding of the duties and responsibilities of the role.

Prepare questions: Prepare a list of informed questions about the role, such as what the day-to-day responsibilities are, what the company culture is like, and what the long-term goals are for the role.

Show enthusiasm: During the interview, show enthusiasm for the role and explain why you are interested in the job requirements. Demonstrate that you have a clear understanding of what the role entails and what you can bring to the company.

By having a clear understanding of the job requirements, you will show the interviewer that you are a well-prepared and motivated candidate, and increase your chances of making a positive impression.

Not Asking Questions

Not asking questions during an interview is another common mistake. Asking questions is a great way to show that you are engaged and interested in the role and the company, and can help you gain valuable information. Here are some tips for avoiding this mistake:

Prepare questions: Before the interview, prepare a list of informed questions about the company, the role, and the interview process.

Ask open-ended questions: Ask open-ended questions that allow the interviewer to provide more

Preparing for Common Interview Questions

Behavioral questions

Behavioral questions are a common type of interview question, where the interviewer asks you to describe a specific situation or experience from your past. This type of question is designed to assess your problem-solving abilities, decision-making skills, and communication skills. Here are some tips for preparing for behavioral questions:

Identify relevant experiences: Think about your past experiences and identify situations that demonstrate the skills and qualities the interviewer is looking for.

Prepare a STAR response: The STAR response is a common method for answering behavioral questions, where you describe the Situation, Task, Action, and Result of a particular experience. This method helps you to structure your answer and provide a clear, concise, and compelling example.

Practice: Practice answering behavioral questions with a friend or family member, or in front of a mirror. This will help you to feel more confident and polished when answering these questions in the interview.

By preparing for behavioral questions, you will be able to demonstrate your relevant skills and experiences, and make a strong impression on the interviewer.

Competency-based questions

Competency-based questions are another common type of interview question, where the interviewer asks you about your skills, knowledge, and experience in a specific area. This type of question is designed to assess your technical ability, as well as your approach to problem-solving and decision-making. Here are some tips for preparing for competency-based questions:

Review the job description: Before the interview, review the job description and identify the key competencies required for the role.

Prepare examples: Think about your previous experiences and prepare concrete examples that demonstrate your competencies. Make sure to include details about the situation, your actions, and the results.

Practice: Practice answering competency-based questions with a friend or family member, or in front of a mirror. This will help you to feel more confident and polished when answering these questions in the interview.

By preparing for competency-based questions, you will be able to demonstrate your technical abilities and approach to problem-solving, and make a strong impression on the interviewer.

Situational questions

These are similar to behavioral questions, but they ask you to imagine a hypothetical situation and describe how you would respond. This type of question is designed to assess your problem-solving skills, decision-making abilities, and communication skills. Here are some tips for preparing for situational questions:

Review the job description: Before the interview, review the job description and identify the key competencies and responsibilities required for the role.

Prepare examples: Think about similar situations you have faced in the past and prepare concrete examples that demonstrate your skills and abilities.

Practice: Practice answering situational questions with a friend or family member, or in front of a mirror. This will help you to feel more confident and polished when answering these questions in the interview.

By preparing for situational questions, you will be able to demonstrate your problem-solving skills, decision-making abilities, and communication skills, and make a strong impression on the interviewer.

Role-specific questions

Preparing for Common Interview Questions: Role-Specific Questions

Role-specific questions are questions that are directly related to the job you are applying for. These questions are designed to assess your knowledge and understanding of the job requirements, as well as your experience and skills in a specific area. Here are some tips for preparing for role-specific questions:

Research the company and the job: Before the interview, research the company and the job you are applying for, and familiarize yourself with the requirements and responsibilities of the role.

Prepare examples: Think about your previous experiences and prepare concrete examples that demonstrate your relevant skills and abilities.

Practice: Practice answering role-specific questions with a friend or family member, or in front of a mirror. This will help you to feel more confident and polished when answering these questions in the interview.

By preparing for role-specific questions, you will be able to demonstrate your knowledge and understanding of the job requirements, and make a strong impression on the interviewer.

Salary and benefits questions

Preparing for Common Interview Questions: Salary and Benefits Questions

Salary and benefits questions are often raised during the interview, and it is important to be prepared for them.

Here are some tips for preparing for salary and benefits questions:

Research the market: Before the interview, research the average salary for the job you are applying for in the local market, and have a good understanding of the standard benefits offered by companies in the industry.

Be honest and transparent: When asked about your salary expectations, be honest and transparent about your current salary and your desired salary range. Keep in mind that this information will likely be verified later on in the hiring process.

Consider the whole package: When negotiating salary and benefits, consider the whole package, including the job responsibilities, company culture, growth opportunities, and other benefits.

By preparing for salary and benefits questions, you will be able to demonstrate your knowledge and understanding of the job market, and make a strong impression on the interviewer.

Conclusion: The Importance of Practice and Preparation

The purpose of an interview is for the employer to assess whether a candidate is a good fit for the job and the company. By understanding the employer's perspective and the job requirements, preparing for common interview questions, and mastering interview skills, you can make a strong impression on the interviewer and increase your chances of getting the job.

The key takeaways from this chapter include the importance of researching the company, dressing appropriately, arriving on time, demonstrating positive body language, active listening, and asking informed questions. Additionally, you should avoid being late, dressing inappropriately, being negative or critical of past employers, talking too much or too little, not having a clear understanding of the job requirements, and not asking questions.

The benefits of mastering interview skills include increased confidence, the ability to make a strong impression on the interviewer, and a better chance of getting the job. By following the tips and guidelines outlined in this book, you can improve your interview skills and increase your chances of success.

XI

Giving Presentations

"Presenting with confidence: Sharing knowledge and data with grace and authority."

Importance of Presentation Skills

Presentation skills are a critical aspect of professional and academic success. Whether you're a student making a class presentation or a job seeker making a pitch to a potential employer, the way you present yourself and your ideas can make a big difference in how you are perceived by others.

Effective presentation skills allow you to communicate your ideas clearly and confidently, engage your audience, and persuade them to take action. Whether you're trying to sell a product, educate an audience, or build support for a cause, having strong presentation skills is essential.

In the professional world, effective presentations are increasingly important as people rely on technology to communicate. While email, video conferencing, and other digital tools make it easier to communicate, they can also detract from the impact of your message. When you're giving a presentation in person, you have the opportunity to make a personal connection with your audience, build rapport, and convey your ideas in a way that email or video cannot.

In the academic world, presentations are a common way to share research findings, communicate ideas, and demonstrate knowledge. Whether you're making a class presentation, participating in a student debate, or presenting at a conference, your ability to present your ideas effectively can have a major impact on your academic success.

In addition to professional and academic success, presentation skills also help to build confidence and self-esteem. When you're able to communicate your ideas effectively, you feel more empowered and capable. This can help you in all areas of your life, from personal relationships to your career.

Presentation skills are an important aspect of both professional and academic success. Whether you're a student, a job seeker, or a professional, being able to present your ideas effectively can help you to build your reputation, make a positive impression, and achieve your goals.

The Basics of Presentation Skills:

Understanding Your Audience

One of the key components of effective presentation skills is understanding your audience. This means understanding who they are, what they're interested in, and what they hope to get out of your presentation. When you understand your audience, you're better equipped to create a presentation that resonates with them and achieves your goals.

Here are a few key steps for understanding your audience:

Research your audience: Before you begin creating your presentation, take some time to research your audience. Find out who they are, what they do, and what their interests are. This information can help you tailor your presentation to their needs and interests.

Consider your audience's needs: Think about what your audience hopes to get out of your presentation. Are they looking for information, inspiration, or entertainment? Knowing what your audience wants can help you create a presentation that meets their needs.

Evaluate your audience's level of knowledge: Consider what your audience already knows about the topic of your presentation. If they're already familiar with the subject, you can focus on more advanced concepts and techniques. If they're new to the topic, you may need to start with the basics.

Adapt to your audience: As you're delivering your presentation, be aware of your audience's reactions and adjust your approach accordingly. If you sense that your audience is losing interest, try to find ways to engage them and keep them focused.

By taking the time to understand your audience, you can create a presentation that connects with them, keeps their attention, and achieves your goals. This is a critical step in developing effective presentation skills.

Selecting a Topic and Creating an Outline

Once you have a good understanding of your audience, the next step is to select a topic and create an outline for your presentation. This will help you to structure your ideas, stay focused, and ensure that your presentation is well organized and easy to follow.

Here are a few tips for selecting a topic and creating an outline:

Choose a topic that interests you: Pick a topic that you're passionate about, as this will make it easier for you to stay motivated and engaged throughout the presentation.

The structure of Presentation:

The structure of your presentation is just as important as the content.

The introduction

Introduction is the first impression your audience will have of your presentation, so it's important to make it count. A well-structured presentation should have a clear beginning, middle, and end, with each section serving a specific purpose. The introduction should grab your audience's attention and provide a clear preview of what's to come.

The goal of your introduction is to grab your audience's attention and set the stage for what's to come. Some effective techniques for introducing your presentation include:

Starting with a surprising statistic or interesting story

Asking a thought-provoking question

Providing a clear overview of what you will cover in your presentation

Example:

Consider the example of Rachel, a marketing professional who was asked to give a presentation on the importance of social media in business. Rachel started her presentation with a surprising statistic: "Did you know that over 4 billion people use social media worldwide? That's more than half of the world's population!" This statistic immediately grabbed her audience's attention and set the stage for the rest of her presentation.

The Body:

The body of your presentation should present your main points and supporting information. Make sure to clearly communicate your message, using clear and concise language, visual aids, and supporting examples. It's also important to maintain a consistent tone and pace throughout your presentation.

Example:

In her presentation on the importance of social media in business, Rachel presented the following main points:

The benefits of using social media for businesses, including increased brand awareness, customer engagement, and the ability to reach a wider audience.

The different types of social media platforms, including Facebook, Instagram, Twitter, and LinkedIn, and how each platform can be used for different purposes.

The importance of having a consistent brand voice and presence across all social media platforms.

Throughout her presentation, Rachel used visual aids, such as slides and graphs, to reinforce her message, and provided real-life examples to illustrate her points.

The Conclusion:

The conclusion of your presentation should summarize the key takeaways and provide a call to action. The goal of your conclusion is to leave a lasting impression on your audience and inspire them to take action. Some effective techniques for concluding your presentation include:

Summarizing the main points of your presentation

Providing a call to action, such as asking your audience to take a specific step or share their thoughts

Ending with a memorable quote or thought-provoking statement

Example:

In her conclusion, Rachel summarized the main points of her presentation and provided a call to action. She said: "In conclusion, social media is a powerful tool for businesses, allowing them to reach a wider audience, increase brand awareness, and engage with customers. I encourage you to start exploring the different social media platforms and finding ways to incorporate them into your business strategy."

Consider your audience: Make sure the topic is relevant and of interest to your audience. You want to choose a topic that will resonate with them and meet their needs.

Create an outline: Once you've selected a topic, create an outline for your presentation. This will help you organize your thoughts and ensure that your presentation flows logically from one point to the next.

Keep it simple: When creating your outline, keep it simple and straightforward. You don't want to overload your audience with information, so focus on the most important points and keep the outline concise.

Use visuals: Consider incorporating visuals into your presentation to help illustrate your points and keep your audience engaged.

By selecting a topic and creating an outline, you'll have a roadmap to follow as you prepare and deliver your presentation. This will help you stay focused and organized, and ensure that your presentation is well received by your audience.

In conclusion, structuring your presentation is a critical part of its success. By having a clear introduction, body, and conclusion, you can ensure that your presentation is well organized, easy to follow, and leaves a lasting impression on your audience.

Preparation and rehearsal

Once you've selected a topic and created an outline, it's time to prepare and rehearse your presentation. This is an important step in developing effective presentation skills, as it will help you refine your message and build confidence in your delivery.

Here are a few tips for preparing and rehearsing your presentation:

Know your material: Make sure you have a thorough understanding of the topic you're presenting. Research and gather any additional information you need to support your points.

Rehearse: Rehearse your presentation several times, both in front of a mirror and in front of a test audience. This will help you get comfortable with your material and identify areas where you need to improve.

Use visual aids: Consider using visual aids such as slides, videos, or props to help illustrate your points and keep your audience engaged. Make sure these visual aids are well-prepared and professional looking.

Timing: Pay attention to timing as you rehearse. Make sure you're delivering your presentation at a pace that's comfortable for you and your audience, and that you have enough time to cover all of the important points.

Practice active listening: As you rehearse, pay attention to your body language, facial expressions, and tone of voice. These are important components of effective presentation skills, and practicing active listening can help you become more aware of your nonverbal cues.

Anticipating questions and preparing answers

Preparation is key when it comes to giving presentations, and one aspect of preparation that is often overlooked is anticipating questions and preparing answers. This can be especially important in professional settings where your audience may have specific questions or concerns that they want addressed.

One effective way to anticipate questions is to think about what information your audience is likely to want to know, based on your topic and the specific context of your presentation. For example, if you are giving a presentation about a new project at work, you might expect questions about the timeline, budget, and expected outcomes.

Another way to anticipate questions is to think about any potential objections or challenges that your audience might have. For example, if you are giving a presentation about a new product, you might expect questions about how it compares to similar products on the market, or about the potential downsides.

Once you have identified the types of questions that you are likely to receive, it is important to prepare thoughtful, well-informed answers. This will help you feel more confident and in control during your presentation, and it will also demonstrate to your audience that you have thoroughly thought through the issues and are well-prepared to address their concerns.

It is also a good idea to practice answering these questions in advance, either on your own or with a colleague or friend who can play the role of an audience member. This will help you refine your responses and become more comfortable with the give-and-take of a Q&A session.

Anticipating potential questions and preparing answers is an important aspect of effective presentation preparation, and one that should not be overlooked. By anticipating the types of questions that your audience might have and preparing thoughtful, well-informed answers, you can build confidence and demonstrate your expertise, and help ensure the success of your presentation.

By preparing and rehearsing your presentation, you'll be better equipped to deliver a confident and engaging performance. This will help you make a positive impression on your audience and achieve your goals

Visual Aids and Props

Visual aids and props can be powerful tools for enhancing your presentation skills. They can help you illustrate your points, keep your audience engaged, and reinforce your message.

Here are a few tips for using visual aids and props effectively:

Choose wisely: Choose visual aids and props that are relevant to your topic and appropriate for your audience. Make sure they support your message and don't distract from it.

Make them professional: Make sure your visual aids and props are well-prepared and professional looking. This will enhance your credibility and help you make a positive impression on your audience.

Use visual aids to illustrate points: Use visual aids, such as slides or videos, to help illustrate your points and keep your audience engaged. Make sure the visual aids are clear and easy to follow, and that they reinforce your message.

Incorporate props: Consider using props, such as physical objects or demonstrations, to help illustrate your points and make your presentation more interactive. Just make sure the props are easy to handle and that you've rehearsed using them before the presentation.

Practice using visual aids and props: Practice using your visual aids and props during your rehearsals. This will help you become more comfortable with them and ensure that they're integrated smoothly into your presentation.

By incorporating visual aids and props into your presentation, you'll be able to engage your audience, reinforce your message, and enhance your overall presentation skills. Just make sure to choose them wisely and use them effectively to achieve the best results.

Creating Effective PowerPoint (PPT) Presentations

PowerPoint is a popular tool for creating presentations, and when used effectively, it can be a powerful tool for enhancing your message and engaging your audience. Here are some tips for creating effective PowerPoint presentations:

Background and font

When selecting a background and font for your PowerPoint presentation, it is important to consider readability and professionalism.

For the background, choose a simple, clean design that complements your content and font. Avoid using busy patterns or background images that may be distracting to your audience. Opt for neutral colors, such as white or light gray, that won't take away from your content.

In terms of font, select a typeface that is easy to read and professional. Sans-serif fonts, such as Arial or Calibri, are often recommended for presentations as they are easy to read on a screen. The font size should be large enough to be easily read by everyone in the room, typically around 24-32 points.

Additionally, choose a font color that is easy to read and complement the background. Avoid using too many colors, as this can be distracting to your audience. Stick to a neutral palette of black, white, and grays, and only use accent colors sparingly to highlight important information.

Number of slides:

When creating a PowerPoint presentation, it's important to be mindful of the number of slides you include. Too many slides can overwhelm your audience and make it difficult for them to follow along. On the other hand, too few slides can leave your audience feeling unsatisfied and without a complete understanding of your message.

As a general rule, aim for one slide per minute of presentation time. This gives you enough time to effectively present the information on each slide and keep the audience engaged. If you have a lot of information to present, consider breaking it up into smaller, more manageable chunks.

Additionally, keep each slide simple and focused on a single message or idea. This helps ensure that your audience is able to retain and understand the information you're presenting.

In conclusion, the number of slides in your PowerPoint presentation should be kept to a minimum, while still providing enough information to effectively communicate your message to your audience.

Keep the number of slides to a minimum. Ideally, aim for one slide per minute of presentation time. Too many slides can overwhelm your audience and make it difficult for them to follow along.

Font color:

The font color you choose for your PowerPoint presentation can have a big impact on its overall effectiveness. The right font color can help draw attention to important information, while the wrong color can make it difficult for your audience to read and understand your content.

When choosing a font color, consider the background color and overall design of your slides. Opt for font colors that provide good contrast with the background, such as black or dark gray on a white or light gray background.

It's also important to keep font color consistent throughout your presentation. This helps to create a professional and polished look, and makes it easier for your audience to follow along.

Avoid using too many different font colors, as this can be distracting and make your presentation appear cluttered. Stick to a neutral palette of black, white, and grays, and only use accent colors sparingly to highlight important information.

The font color you choose for your PowerPoint presentation should be easy to read, complement the background, and consistent throughout the presentation.

Mistakes

There are several common mistakes that people make when creating PowerPoint presentations, and avoiding these mistakes can help ensure that your presentation is effective and well-received.

Overloading slides with information: Try to limit the amount of text on each slide, and instead use images, charts, and diagrams to communicate your message.

Poor font choice: Use clear and legible fonts, and make sure that the font size is large enough for your audience to read from a distance.

Inconsistent formatting: Keep the overall design of your slides consistent, and make sure that elements such as font, color, and images are used consistently throughout your presentation.

Ignoring the audience: Make sure your presentation is designed to engage your audience and keep them interested, rather than just reading off of slides.

Relying too heavily on slides: Remember that your slides are there to support your presentation, not to carry it. Try to spend more time speaking and less time reading from your slides.

Not proofreading: Check your presentation for typos, grammatical errors, and other mistakes before presenting.

Ignoring the flow: Make sure your presentation flows logically and clearly, with a clear beginning, middle, and end.

Avoiding these common mistakes can help ensure that your PowerPoint presentation is effective and well-received by your audience.

Content per slide:

The content of each slide in a PowerPoint presentation is crucial to its success. Here are some tips for ensuring that the content of each slide is effective:

Keep it simple: Try to limit the amount of text on each slide, and instead use images, charts, and diagrams to communicate your message.

Focus on one main message per slide: Each slide should have a clear, focused message that supports your overall presentation.

Use visual aids: Use images, charts, and diagrams to help illustrate your message and make it more engaging for your audience.

Be concise: Use short, concise sentences and bullet points to help your audience quickly understand the key points of your presentation.

Highlight important information: Use font colors, bold text, and other formatting techniques to help your audience quickly identify the most important information on each slide.

Use consistency: Keep the overall design of your slides consistent, and make sure that elements such as font, color, and images are used consistently throughout your presentation.

Avoid clutter: Avoid using too many different elements on each slide, as this can make your presentation appear cluttered and confusing to your audience.

The content of each slide in a PowerPoint presentation should be simple, focused, concise, and visually engaging. By following these tips, you can ensure that your presentation is effective and well-received by your audience.

Images

Images can be a powerful tool in enhancing the impact of your presentation. Here are some tips for using images effectively:

Choose relevant images: Make sure that the images you use are relevant to your presentation topic and support your message.

Use high-quality images: Use high-resolution images that are clear and visually appealing to ensure that they have the maximum impact.

Use images to illustrate your message: Use images to help illustrate your message and make it more engaging for your audience.

Use images to create visual interest: Use images to break up large blocks of text and add visual interest to your presentation.

Use images to support data: Use charts, graphs, and other data visualization tools to help explain complex data or concepts.

Be mindful of image size: Be mindful of the size of the images you use, as large images can slow down your presentation or cause it to appear cluttered.

Be aware of copyright: Make sure that you have the rights to use any images that you include in your presentation, or choose images that are available for free or for commercial use.

Images can be a powerful tool in enhancing the impact of your presentation. By choosing relevant, high-quality images and using them effectively, you can help ensure that your presentation is well-received by your audience.

Transitions and animations

Transitions and animations can help add visual interest and professional polish to your presentation. Here are some tips for using transitions and animations effectively:

Use transitions judiciously: Too many transitions can be distracting and take away from the content of your presentation. Use transitions sparingly and only when they add to your message.

Choose appropriate transitions: Choose transitions that complement your presentation's style and tone. Simple, smooth transitions are often the most effective.

Use animations to emphasize key points: Use animations to draw your audience's attention to important information or concepts.

Use animations to make complex information easier to understand: Use animations to help explain complex information or data, such as graphs or flow charts.

Be mindful of animation length: Be mindful of the length of your animations, as long or repetitive animations can become boring for your audience.

Test your animations: Make sure to test your animations thoroughly before your presentation to ensure that they work as intended and do not cause any technical issues.

Transitions and animations can add visual interest and professional polish to your presentation. By using them judiciously and choosing appropriate transitions and animations, you can help make your presentation more engaging and effective for your audience.

By following these tips, you can create effective PowerPoint presentations that engage and inform your audience, and help you achieve your presentation goals.

Starting Your Presentation

Introduction:

The introduction of your presentation is crucial as it sets the tone and captures the audience's attention. Here are some tips for starting your presentation effectively:

Greet your audience

Greeting your audience is an important part of starting your presentation. Here are some tips for greeting your audience effectively:

Be friendly and professional: Start your presentation with a friendly and professional greeting that sets a positive tone for the rest of your presentation.

Address the audience by name: If possible, address the audience by their name, for example, "Good morning, everyone" or "Good afternoon, [name of the organization or group]".

Acknowledge the occasion: If your presentation is part of a larger event, acknowledge the occasion and thank the organizers for having you as a speaker.

Show appreciation: Express appreciation for your audience's time and interest in your presentation.

By greeting your audience effectively, you can build rapport, set a positive tone, and establish a connection with your audience. This can help make your presentation more engaging and effective.

Establish credibility

Establishing credibility is an important part of starting your presentation, as it helps your audience to trust and believe in what you have to say. Here are some tips for establishing credibility:

Highlight your expertise: If appropriate, highlight your qualifications, experience, and expertise in the topic you're presenting on.

Use credentials: If you have any relevant credentials, such as a degree, certification, or professional experience, mention them briefly.

Provide references: If you have cited any research, studies, or experts in your presentation, provide references to support your credibility.

Use testimonials: If you have received any testimonials from clients, colleagues, or industry leaders, consider using them to establish your credibility.

By establishing credibility, you can demonstrate to your audience that you are knowledgeable and trustworthy, which can help to make your presentation more persuasive and effective.

Preview your presentation:

Previewing the main points of your presentation can help to give your audience a clear understanding of what to expect. This helps to set their expectations and provides them with a roadmap of your presentation. When previewing the main points, it's important to highlight the key themes, takeaways, and objectives of your presentation. This can be done by briefly mentioning each of the key topics you will be covering, and how they are relevant to your overall message. By doing so, you can create a smooth transition into the body of your presentation and help to keep your audience engaged and focused.

Get their attention

Getting your audience's attention is crucial to the success of your presentation. Here are some tips for getting your audience's attention:

Start with a hook: Begin your presentation with a compelling hook that grabs your audience's attention and keeps them engaged. This could be a surprising statistic, a provocative question, or a personal story related to the topic.

Use visual aids: Use visual aids, such as images, graphs, or videos, to help illustrate your points and keep your audience's attention focused on your presentation.

Make eye contact: Make eye contact with members of your audience throughout your presentation to help maintain their attention and build a connection with them.

Vary your delivery: Vary your delivery by using different tones, pauses, and gestures to help keep your audience engaged and focused.By getting your audience's attention, you can ensure that they are engaged and invested in your presentation, which can help to make your presentation more impactful and memorable.

Build rapport

Building rapport with your audience is important for creating a positive and productive atmosphere during your presentation. Here are some tips for building rapport:

Show interest in your audience: Ask questions, engage in conversation, and make an effort to understand your audience's perspectives and needs.

Personalize your presentation: Use personal anecdotes, stories, and examples that are relevant to your audience to help build a connection with them.

Use humor: Use humor appropriately to help lighten the mood and build rapport with your audience.

Be yourself: Be authentic, genuine, and sincere in your presentation to help build a rapport with your audience.

By building rapport with your audience, you can create a supportive and engaging environment that can help to make your presentation more effective and enjoyable for everyone involved.

By starting your presentation effectively, you can grab your audience's attention and set the stage for a successful and engaging presentation.

Delivering Your Presentation:

Body Language and Non-Verbal Communication

Body language and non-verbal communication are important components of effective presentation skills. They can help you convey your message and connect with your audience, even if you're not speaking.

Here are a few tips for using body language and non-verbal communication effectively:

Be aware of your body language: Pay attention to your posture, gestures, and facial expressions as you deliver your presentation. Make sure they're open, confident, and appropriate for the situation.

Make eye contact: Make eye contact with your audience throughout your presentation. This will help you establish a connection with them and convey confidence and credibility.

Use gestures: Use gestures to emphasize your points and keep your audience engaged. Just make sure they're natural and appropriate for the situation.

Use facial expressions: Use facial expressions to convey your emotions and reinforce your message. Smile, nod, or raise your eyebrows to show that you're engaged and interested in what you're presenting.

Be mindful of your tone of voice: Pay attention to your tone of voice as you deliver your presentation. Make sure it's clear, confident, and appropriate for the situation.

By being aware of your body language and non-verbal communication, you'll be able to engage your audience, reinforce your message, and convey confidence and credibility. This will help you make a positive impression on your audience and achieve your goals.

Voice projection and modulation

Voice projection and modulation are important components of effective presentation skills. They can help you deliver your message clearly and with impact, and keep your audience engaged.

Here are a few tips for using voice projection and modulation effectively:

Project your voice: Make sure your voice is loud enough to be heard by everyone in the room. Speak clearly and articulate your words well to ensure that your message is understood.

Modulate your voice: Vary the tone, pitch, and pace of your voice to keep your audience engaged. Use different tones to emphasize different points, and vary the pace of your speech to match the content of your presentation.

Warm up your voice: Take time to warm up your voice before your presentation. This will help you deliver your message more effectively and avoid any vocal strain.

Practice good breathing techniques: Good breathing techniques will help you project your voice and maintain control over your delivery. Take deep breaths and speak from your diaphragm to achieve the best results.

Use microphone if necessary: If you're delivering your presentation in a large room or to a large audience, consider using a microphone to help amplify your voice. Make sure to test the microphone and adjust the volume levels to ensure that your voice can be heard clearly.

By focusing on voice projection and modulation, you'll be able to deliver your message effectively and keep your audience engaged. This will help you make a positive impression on your audience and achieve your goals.

Dealing with nervousness and anxiety

Nervousness and anxiety are common feelings for many people when it comes to giving presentations. However, with the right preparation and mindset, you can learn to manage these feelings and deliver a confident and effective presentation.

Here are a few tips for dealing with nervousness and anxiety:

Prepare thoroughly: Preparation is key to reducing nervousness and anxiety. Make sure you know your material well and practice your presentation several times to build confidence.

Get organized: Make sure you have all the materials you need for your presentation and that you know the order in which you'll present them. This will help you feel more in control and reduce anxiety.

Visualize success: Visualize yourself delivering a successful presentation. Imagine yourself speaking confidently, making eye contact, and engaging your audience. This can help to build confidence and reduce anxiety.

Practice deep breathing: Take deep breaths before your presentation to calm your nerves and help you focus. This can also help to slow your heart rate and reduce physical symptoms of anxiety.

Embrace nervousness: Remember that it's normal to feel nervous before a presentation. Embrace your nervousness as a sign that you're taking your presentation seriously and that you're committed to delivering your best.

By following these tips, you can learn to manage your nervousness and anxiety and deliver a confident and effective presentation. With practice, you'll find that you become more confident and comfortable with public speaking, and that your presentations become easier and more enjoyable.

Handling questions and feedback

Handling questions and feedback is an important part of delivering an effective presentation. It's an opportunity for you to engage with your audience, address their concerns, and further explain your ideas.

Here are a few tips for handling questions and feedback:

Encourage questions:

Anticipating potential questions and preparing answers in advance can help you feel more confident and in control during your presentation. Consider common questions that might arise based on your topic and research, and prepare concise and well-structured answers that clearly communicate your message.

It's important to encourage questions and feedback from your audience as it helps to engage them and also helps you to understand their perspectives.

Being prepared for common questions and objections can help you to feel more confident during your presentation.

It's also important to use questions and feedback to improve your presentation, this shows that you value the opinions of your audience and want to deliver the best presentation possible.

Responding to questions and feedback with grace and professionalism is also crucial, this shows that you are approachable and professional.

When encouraging questions and feedback, it's important to create a welcoming and inclusive environment. This can be achieved by making eye contact with your audience, using open body language, and using a friendly and approachable tone of voice.

Building a rapport with your audience through interaction can also help to make your presentation more enjoyable for both you and your audience.

Encourage your audience to ask questions by leaving time for Q&A at the end of your presentation. This shows that you're open to feedback and that you value your audience's input.

Listen actively: When someone asks a question, listen actively and make sure you understand their question before answering. This shows that you're respectful and engaged with your audience.

Answer clearly: Answer questions clearly and concisely. Make sure you address the main points of the question and provide relevant information.

Be honest: If you don't know the answer to a question, be honest and say so. Offer to follow up with the information later if you're able to.

Respond to feedback: Respond to feedback in a professional and respectful manner. Acknowledge any constructive criticism and consider it as an opportunity to improve your presentation skills.

When receiving feedback, it's important to stay calm, listen actively, and take the time to understand the perspective of your audience. If someone provides criticism or concerns, try to see it as an opportunity to improve and grow, rather than a personal attack.

Respond to feedback in a respectful and professional manner, and show appreciation for the time and effort your audience took to provide feedback.

By handling questions and feedback effectively, you'll be able to engage with your audience, address their concerns, and deliver an even more effective presentation. This will help you build a positive relationship with your audience and achieve your goals.

Advanced Presentation Techniques

Storytelling in presentations

Storytelling is a powerful tool that can be used to engage and captivate your audience. When used effectively, storytelling can help you bring your ideas to life and make your presentation more memorable.

Here are a few tips for using storytelling in your presentations:

Find a relevant story: Find a story that is relevant to your presentation topic. The story should illustrate your point and help your audience understand your ideas.

Make it personal: Personal stories are often more engaging than generic stories. If possible, find a personal story that relates to your topic and share it with your audience.

Use vivid detail: Use vivid detail to make your story come to life. Describe the setting, the characters, and the emotions involved in the story.

Practice your delivery: Practice your storytelling skills by rehearsing your story several times. Pay attention to your tone, pace, and delivery to ensure that your story is engaging and effective.

Keep it concise: Keep your story concise and to the point. A well-told story can be more powerful than a lengthy explanation.

By using storytelling effectively in your presentations, you'll be able to engage your audience, illustrate your ideas, and make your presentation more memorable. Storytelling is a valuable tool for making your presentations more effective and enjoyable for your audience.

Using Humor and Anecdotes

Humor and anecdotes can be powerful tools for engaging and entertaining your audience. When used effectively, humor and anecdotes can help you connect with your audience, lighten the mood, and make your presentation more memorable.

Here are a few tips for using humor and anecdotes in your presentations:

Know your audience: Before incorporating humor or anecdotes into your presentation, consider your audience. What type of humor is appropriate and what anecdotes will resonate with your audience?

Make it relevant: Make sure your humor or anecdotes are relevant to your presentation topic. The humor should illustrate your point and help your audience understand your ideas.

Use timing effectively: Timing is key when it comes to humor. Make sure your humor or anecdotes are delivered at the right time to maximize their impact.

Keep it light: Don't overdo the humor or anecdotes. A well-placed joke or anecdote can be effective, but too much humor can detract from your presentation.

Rehearse: Rehearse your humor and anecdotes several times to make sure they are delivered effectively. Pay attention to your timing, tone, and delivery to ensure that your humor and anecdotes are engaging and effective.

By using humor and anecdotes effectively in your presentations, you'll be able to engage your audience, lighten the mood, and make your presentation more memorable. Humor and anecdotes are valuable tools for making your presentations more effective and enjoyable for your audience.

Creating Engaging and Interactive Presentations

Interactivity is a key element in making your presentation engaging and memorable. When you involve your audience in the presentation, they are more likely to be invested in the content and retain the information.

Here are a few tips for creating engaging and interactive presentations:

Ask questions: Encourage audience participation by asking questions throughout your presentation. This not only makes the presentation more interactive, but it also helps you gauge your audience's understanding of the material.

Use interactive elements: Use interactive elements, such as polls or quizzes, to engage your audience and make your presentation more dynamic.

Encourage discussion: Encourage audience members to share their thoughts and opinions on the topic. This can be done through open-ended questions, small group discussions, or interactive activities.

Use visual aids: Use visual aids, such as slides, videos, or images, to support your presentation and make it more interactive.

Be responsive: Be responsive to your audience during the presentation. If they ask questions or make comments, take the time to engage with them and address their concerns.

By creating engaging and interactive presentations, you'll be able to hold your audience's attention, keep them invested in the content, and make your presentation more memorable. Interactivity is a valuable tool for making your presentations more effective and enjoyable for your audience.

Common Mistakes to Avoid

Overloading with Information

One of the biggest mistakes presenters make is trying to cover too much information in a single presentation. This can lead to an overwhelming and confusing experience for your audience, and they are likely to forget the majority of what was covered.

Here are a few tips for avoiding this mistake:

Be selective: Be selective about the information you include in your presentation. Focus on the most important and relevant information and leave out the rest.

Keep it simple: Make sure your presentation is simple and easy to follow. Use clear and concise language, and keep your slides uncluttered.

Prioritize information: Prioritize the information in your presentation, starting with the most important points and working your way down to the less important information.

Use visual aids: Use visual aids, such as slides or images, to support your presentation and help you avoid overwhelming your audience with too much information.

Practice: Rehearse your presentation several times to make sure you are covering the information in an organized and concise manner.

By avoiding the mistake of overloading your audience with information, you'll be able to deliver a clear and effective presentation that is easy for your audience to understand and remember.

Lack of Preparation and Rehearsal

Another common mistake that many presenters make is not preparing and rehearsing their presentation adequately. This can lead to a lack of confidence and a poorly structured presentation, which can negatively impact your audience's engagement and understanding of the material.

Here are a few tips for avoiding this mistake:

Plan ahead: Plan your presentation well in advance and create an outline to help you organize your thoughts and content.

Rehearse: Rehearse your presentation several times to ensure that you are comfortable with the material and can deliver the presentation smoothly and confidently.

Time yourself: Time yourself during your rehearsals to ensure that you are keeping within the allotted time for your presentation.

Practice in front of a friend: Practice your presentation in front of a friend or family member to get feedback and make any necessary adjustments.

Be flexible: Be flexible and willing to make changes to your presentation if necessary. It's better to make changes and improvements before the actual presentation rather than during.

By preparing and rehearsing your presentation thoroughly, you'll be able to deliver a confident, well-structured, and engaging presentation that is sure to impress your audience.

Poor body language and eye contact

Body language and eye contact play an important role in the success of a presentation, as they can impact your audience's perception of you and the message you are trying to convey. Poor body language and eye contact can detract from the effectiveness of your presentation and make you appear unconfident or uninterested in your topic.

Here are a few tips for avoiding this mistake:

Practice good posture: Stand up straight and maintain good posture during your presentation. This will help you appear confident and in control.

Use gestures: Use natural gestures to emphasize your points and engage your audience. Avoid excessive or unnatural gestures, as they can be distracting.

Make eye contact: Make eye contact with your audience throughout your presentation. This helps to establish a connection and shows that you are engaged and confident.

Avoid fidgeting: Avoid fidgeting, such as tapping your foot or shuffling your feet, as it can be distracting to your audience.

Smile: Smile and maintain a positive and friendly demeanor throughout your presentation. This will help to put your audience at ease and make your presentation more engaging.

By avoiding poor body language and eye contact, you'll be able to deliver a confident and engaging presentation that connects with your audience and effectively conveys your message.

Speaking in a Monotone Voice

Speaking in a monotone voice can make a presentation dull and unengaging, which can detract from the effectiveness of your message. A monotone voice can also make you appear uninterested in your topic and put your audience to sleep.

Here are a few tips for avoiding this mistake:

Practice inflection: Practice speaking with inflection and varying your pitch to keep your audience engaged and interested.

Use pauses: Use pauses effectively to give your audience time to process your message and to add emphasis to your points.

Speak at a moderate pace: Speak at a moderate pace that is easy for your audience to follow, but not so slow that they get bored.

Vary your volume: Vary your volume to add emphasis and to keep your audience interested.

Use tone: Use tone to add emotion and to convey your message more effectively.

By avoiding speaking in a monotone voice, you'll be able to deliver a dynamic and engaging presentation that effectively conveys your message and keeps your audience interested.

Final thoughts and recommendations

Presentation skills are essential for success in a variety of settings, whether you are a student, jobseeker, or professional. By understanding your audience, preparing and rehearsing effectively, and using advanced techniques to engage and interact with your audience, you can deliver presentations that are effective, memorable, and impactful.

Here are some final thoughts and recommendations for improving your presentation skills:

Practice, practice, practice: The more you practice, the more confident and effective you will become as a presenter.

Get feedback: Seek feedback from others on your presentations to identify areas for improvement and continue to grow and develop your skills.

Stay current: Stay up to date with the latest presentation trends and technologies to continue to enhance your presentations and keep your audience engaged.

Be yourself: Be authentic and let your personality shine through in your presentations to connect with your audience and create a memorable experience.

Have fun: Enjoy the process of preparing and delivering presentations. Remember that you are sharing your knowledge and ideas with others, and the more you enjoy the process, the more your audience will enjoy your presentation.

Presentation skills are a valuable asset that can help you achieve success in your personal and professional life. By following these recommendations and continually practicing and improving your skills, you can become a confident and effective presenter and make a positive impact on your audience.

Call to action for readers to start practicing and improving their presentation skills

Now that you have a better understanding of the basics and advanced techniques of presentation skills, it's time to put your knowledge into practice. Don't wait any longer to start improving your skills and making a positive impact on your audience.

Here's what you can do right now to start improving your presentation skills:

Choose a topic: Select a topic you are passionate about and want to present on.

Create an outline: Use the information you learned in the this chapter to create a detailed outline for your presentation.

Prepare and rehearse: Take the time to prepare and rehearse your presentation, paying close attention to your body language, voice projection, and use of visual aids and props.

Deliver your presentation: Find a willing audience, whether it be friends, family, classmates, or colleagues, and deliver your presentation.

Seek feedback: Ask for feedback from your audience and use it to improve your skills for future presentations.

Don't be afraid to make mistakes, as they are an important part of the learning process. Remember, the more you practice, the better you will become. So, take the first step and start improving your presentation skills today!

Here is a section for students presenting their project work or seminars:

Guide for Students Presenting Their Thesis or Project Work

Know your material

Yes, knowing your material is an important aspect of presenting effectively. This means taking the time to thoroughly research and understand your topic, and being familiar with the key points and arguments you want to make. Having a deep understanding of your material will help you to present with confidence and competence, and respond to questions and feedback from your audience. It's also a good idea to have backup information in case you need to refer to it during your presentation. Preparation is key to delivering a successful presentation, and knowing your material is a critical part of that preparation.

Plan and prepare

Planning and preparation are crucial elements of a successful presentation. This includes determining your objective and target audience, selecting an appropriate topic and creating an outline, and deciding on the best way to present your material (e.g. through a slide presentation, poster, or live demonstration). It's also important to consider how to best engage your audience and make your presentation memorable.

In terms of preparation, it's a good idea to rehearse your presentation several times, both in front of a mirror and with a friend or family member. This will help you to identify and address any issues with your delivery, such as nervous habits or unclear transitions between slides. You should also familiarize yourself with the equipment you will be using and ensure that you have any necessary props or materials on hand.

Finally, it's important to arrive early on the day of your presentation so that you have time to set up, test the equipment, and mentally prepare yourself. With thorough planning and preparation, you'll be well-positioned to deliver a confident and effective presentation.

Use visual aids effectively

Visual aids, such as slides, posters, or props, can be powerful tools for enhancing the impact of your presentation. However, it's important to use them effectively in order to avoid distracting from your message or overwhelming your audience with information.

When creating visual aids, consider the following tips:

Keep it simple: Use clear, simple graphics and limited text to reinforce your key points and make your presentation easier to follow.

Use color wisely: Color can help to emphasize important information, but be careful not to use too many colors or overly bright hues that can be distracting.

Use images effectively: Images can be a great way to break up text and add visual interest to your presentation, but make sure they are relevant to your topic and of high quality.

Avoid clutter: Avoid including too much information on a single slide or poster, as this can make it difficult for your audience to focus and retain the information.

Be consistent: Ensure that your visual aids have a consistent look and feel, with the same font, color scheme, and formatting throughout.

By using visual aids effectively, you can enhance the impact of your presentation and make it more memorable for your audience.

Be organized

Organization is key to a successful presentation. Whether you're presenting a project for a class or giving a seminar as part of your academic work, having a well-structured presentation can help you effectively communicate your ideas and keep your audience engaged.

Here are a few tips for being organized during your presentation:

Have a clear outline: Before you begin, make sure you have a clear and well-organized outline of the key points you want to cover. This can help you stay on track and ensure that your presentation flows smoothly.

Use clear transitions: When transitioning from one point to the next, use clear language and gestures to signal to your audience that you are moving on. This can help to keep your presentation organized and prevent confusion.

Be mindful of timing: Make sure you have enough time to cover all of your key points and leave time for questions and discussion at the end.

Keep it concise: Try to keep your presentation as concise as possible, avoiding extraneous information or lengthy explanations that can distract from your main points.

By being well-organized, you can create a presentation that is both effective and engaging for your audience.

Engage with your audience

Engaging with your audience is a key aspect of a successful presentation. By connecting with your audience, you can build rapport, establish credibility, and get your message across more effectively.

Here are some tips for engaging with your audience during your presentation:

Make eye contact: Making eye contact with your audience helps to establish a connection and demonstrates your confidence and credibility.

Use body language: Use your body language to convey your message and engage with your audience. Stand up straight, make gestures, and use facial expressions to emphasize your points.

Involve your audience: Ask questions, solicit feedback, and encourage participation from your audience. This can help to keep them engaged and invested in your presentation.

Be relatable: Use anecdotes, humor, and personal stories to connect with your audience and make your presentation more relatable and engaging.

By engaging with your audience, you can create a dynamic and interactive presentation that will leave a lasting impression and help you achieve your goals.

Anticipating Potential Questions and Preparing Answers:

Presenting a thesis or project work in front of classmates or teachers can be a daunting task, especially if you're not prepared. One of the keys to a successful presentation is being able to anticipate potential questions and prepare answers. This will not only demonstrate your knowledge and mastery of the subject matter, but also give you confidence and help you feel more relaxed during the presentation.

Here are some tips to help you anticipate potential questions and prepare answers for your thesis or project presentation:

Read and study the material thoroughly: Make sure you have a thorough understanding of the material you're presenting. This will help you answer any questions that may come up during the presentation.

Identify key points: Determine the most important points of your presentation and focus on them. This will help you stay on track and ensure that you cover all the key points during your presentation.

Consider the audience: Think about who your audience is and what they might want to know. Try to anticipate their questions and prepare answers that are specific to their interests and needs.

Research the topic: Do some research on the topic you're presenting to expand your knowledge and be better prepared to answer questions.

Review past presentations: Look at past presentations on similar topics to see what questions were asked and how they were answered. This will give you an idea of what to expect and help you prepare.

Practice, practice, practice: Rehearse your presentation multiple times so that you feel more confident and prepared. During these rehearsals, try to answer any potential questions that may come up during the presentation.

Prepare backup material: Have backup information and supporting materials ready in case you need to reference them during the presentation.

By anticipating potential questions and preparing answers, you'll be better equipped to give a successful and confident presentation. Your audience will appreciate your effort and your preparation will help you feel more relaxed and at ease during the presentation.

Practice and refine

Practice and refinement are critical components of a successful presentation. It takes time and effort to develop the skills and confidence needed to deliver a polished and engaging presentation.

Here are some tips for practicing and refining your presentation skills:

Rehearse: The more you practice your presentation, the more comfortable you will feel when it comes time to deliver it. Try to rehearse in a setting that simulates the actual presentation environment as closely as possible.

Seek feedback: Ask friends, family, or classmates to listen to your presentation and provide feedback. This can help you identify areas for improvement and make changes to enhance the overall quality of your presentation.

Use visual aids: Visual aids such as slides or props can help to reinforce your key points and keep your audience engaged. Make sure to practice using them during your rehearsal to ensure a smooth and seamless delivery.

Watch and learn from others: Attend presentations by other students, professionals, or experts in your field. Observe what they do well and what you can learn from their presentation style and techniques.

By practicing and refining your presentation skills, you can become more confident and effective in communicating your ideas and sharing your knowledge with others.

By following these tips, students can deliver effective and impactful presentations for their academic coursework or degree projects, and demonstrate their knowledge and skills to their instructors, peers, and future employers.

Overcoming Fear and Anxiety for Student Presentations

Giving a presentation as a student, whether it's a seminar, a project presentation, or a class presentation, can be a nerve-wracking experience. However, with proper preparation and a few strategies, you can overcome your fear and anxiety and deliver an effective presentation.

Here are some tips for overcoming fear and anxiety for student presentations:

Know your material: Be well-prepared and knowledgeable about your topic. This will help you feel more confident and reduce anxiety.

Plan and practice: Create an outline, practice your delivery, and become familiar with the flow of your presentation. The more you practice, the more comfortable and confident you'll become.

Use visual aids: Utilize visual aids such as slides, props, or demonstrations to support your presentation and keep your audience engaged.

Take deep breaths: Take deep breaths before you begin your presentation to calm your nerves and help you stay focused.

Connect with your audience: Make eye contact, smile, and use body language to connect with your audience and engage them in your presentation.

Handling Questions from Teachers

During a student presentation, it's likely that you'll be asked questions by your teacher or classmates. Being able to answer questions effectively is an important part of delivering a successful presentation.

Here are some tips for handling questions during your presentation:

Listen carefully: Pay close attention to the question and make sure you understand what's being asked before you respond.

Take a moment to think: If you need a moment to think before answering a question, that's okay. Take a deep breath and gather your thoughts before you respond.

Be honest: If you don't know the answer to a question, it's okay to admit it. Offer to find out more information and follow up with the answer later.

Be confident: Answer questions with confidence, using clear and concise language. Your body language should also reflect confidence and poise.

Do's and Don'ts for Student Presentations

Here are some general do's and don'ts for student presentations:
Do's:

- Be prepared and knowledgeable about your topic
- Use visual aids to support your presentation
- Make eye contact with your audience
- Speak clearly and project your voice
- Practice your delivery before the presentation

Don'ts:

- Read from your slides or notes
- Speak too quickly or too slowly
- Use filler words such as "um" or "ah"
- Ignore or dismiss questions from your audience
- Get sidetracked from the main points of your presentation

Opening Your Presentation and Introducing Topics

Starting your presentation off on the right foot is important for engaging your audience and setting the tone for the rest of the presentation. Here are some tips for opening your presentation and introducing your topics:

Greet your audience: Begin by greeting your audience and introducing yourself. This helps to establish a connection and make your audience feel at ease.

Establish credibility: If you have any relevant experience or qualifications, mention them briefly to establish your credibility on the topic.

Grab their attention: Start with an interesting fact, a personal story, or a thought-provoking question to grab the attention of your audience.

Clearly state your objectives: Clearly state the objectives and goals of your presentation to set expectations for your audience.

Provide an overview of your topics: Provide an overview of the topics you'll be covering, and how they fit together to support your overall presentation.

Strategies for managing nervousness and anxiety

Dealing with nervousness and anxiety is a common challenge faced by many students when presenting their projects or seminar work. However, there are various strategies that can be employed to help manage these feelings.

Deep Breathing: Taking deep breaths can help to calm the body and mind before and during the presentation. This technique involves taking slow, deep breaths and counting to 10 while inhaling and exhaling.

Visualization: This technique involves creating a mental image of a calm and successful presentation. Imagine yourself speaking confidently, engaging with the audience, and delivering the material effectively.

Positive Self-Talk: Encouraging yourself with positive affirmations can help to boost your confidence and reduce anxiety. Repeat positive phrases such as "I am prepared and confident" or "I can do this" to help build a positive mental attitude.

Rehearsal: Practicing the presentation can help to build confidence and reduce anxiety. Try to present the material in front of a friend or family member to help build your skills and reduce nervousness.

Get Enough Sleep: Lack of sleep can increase feelings of nervousness and anxiety. Make sure to get enough sleep in the days leading up to the presentation.

Remember, it is normal to feel nervous or anxious when presenting. The key is to find strategies that work best for you to manage these feelings and deliver a confident and engaging presentation.

Tips for building confidence and self-assurance before and during your presentation

Building confidence and self-assurance before and during your presentation can be a key factor in helping to overcome nervousness and anxiety. Here are a few tips that can help you achieve this:

Preparation: Preparation is key in helping you feel confident and self-assured. Make sure to do your research and understand your topic thoroughly. Rehearse your presentation several times to get comfortable with the content and delivery.

Positive self-talk: Your internal dialogue has a big impact on how you feel. Before your presentation, engage in positive self-talk and focus on your strengths and abilities. During the presentation, remind yourself of your successes and skills.

Visualization: Visualize yourself delivering a successful presentation. Imagine yourself speaking with confidence, engaging with your audience, and handling any challenges that come your way.

Deep breathing: Deep breathing can help you calm your nerves and regulate your breathing during the presentation. Try taking slow, deep breaths before you begin and throughout your presentation to help reduce anxiety.

Focus on the present moment: Instead of focusing on the future outcome or past mistakes, focus on the present moment. This will help you stay grounded and focused on delivering a successful presentation.

Engage with your audience: Engaging with your audience is a great way to build confidence and reduce nervousness. Ask questions, make eye contact, and use gestures to connect with your audience.

By following these tips, you can help build confidence and self-assurance and overcome any nervousness or anxiety you may feel during your presentation.

Handling Questions and Feedback

One key aspect of effective presentation skills is the ability to handle questions and feedback from your audience. This can be a daunting task for many students, especially if they are presenting for the first time or speaking about a complex or technical subject.

However, encouraging questions and feedback from your audience can help build engagement and enhance the overall quality of your presentation.

To prepare for questions and feedback, it is important to anticipate what types of questions may be asked. This can be done by reviewing your presentation and identifying any areas that may be unclear or controversial. Additionally, you can research common questions related to your topic and prepare thoughtful and well-informed answers.

When handling challenging questions, it is important to remain calm, confident, and professional. If you are unsure of an answer, it is okay to admit this and offer to look into it further or provide more information at a later time. It is also important to listen actively and avoid becoming defensive or argumentative.

When encouraging questions and feedback, it's important to create a welcoming and inclusive environment. This can be achieved by making eye contact with your audience, using open body language, and using a friendly and approachable tone of voice.

When receiving feedback, it's important to stay calm, listen actively, and take the time to understand the perspective of your audience. If someone provides criticism or concerns, try to see it as an opportunity to improve and grow, rather than a personal attack. Respond to feedback in a respectful and professional manner, and show appreciation for the time and effort your audience took to provide feedback.